Know Your PRESIDENTS and Their WIVES

By GEORGE E. ROSS

Illustrations by SEYMOUR FLEISHMAN

RAND McNALLY & COMPANY

CHICAGO   NEW YORK   SAN FRANCISCO

First printing, January, 1961
Second printing, July, 1961
Third printing, October, 1963
Fourth printing, July, 1965
Fifth printing, February, 1969

Contents

ACKNOWLEDGMENTS

Sources of the photographs of the Presidents and their wives used in this book are gratefully acknowledged as follows:

    Library of Congress Collections: pp. 5, 7, 17, 19, 21, 23, 25, 29, 31, 35, 37, 39, 41, 43, 45, 47, 49, 51, 53, 57, 61.
    The Smithsonian Institution: pp. 9, 13, 15, 33, 59, 63.
    Harris & Ewing: pp. 23, 55, 58, 60, 62, 64, 65, 67.
    Ewing Galloway: pp. 16, 32.
    Wide World Photos, Inc.: pp. 68, 69.
    Special acknowledgment is also made to Mrs. James S. Tate for permission to use the photograph of Margaret Taylor on p. 27.

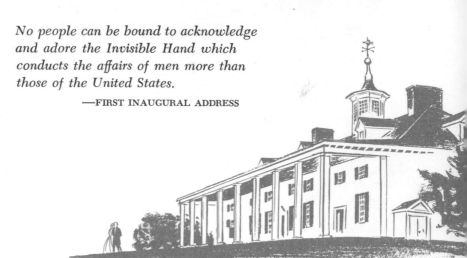

No people can be bound to acknowledge and adore the Invisible Hand which conducts the affairs of men more than those of the United States.

—FIRST INAUGURAL ADDRESS

George Washington

1st President, 1789–1797 — Party: Federalist

BORN: February 22, 1732
BIRTHPLACE: Bridges Creek, Virginia
PARENTS: Augustine and Mary Ball Washington
EDUCATION: At home or at local schools
RELIGION: Episcopalian

OCCUPATIONS: Surveyor; soldier; planter
MARRIED: Martha Dandridge Custis, 1759
AGE AT INAUGURATION: 57
TERMS OF OFFICE: Two (8 years)
DIED: December 14, 1799. Age, 67

FIRST and in many respects the most honored of our Presidents was George Washington, known to all Americans as "the father of his country." Washington was the son of a Virginia planter and received his only formal education at local schools or at home. As a youth he learned surveying, but after he inherited Mount Vernon he became a planter.

Washington began his career in the service of his country as a major in the Virginia militia and was later a colonel under General Braddock during the French and Indian Wars. Respected for his courage, honesty, and sound judgment, he was elected to the Virginia House of Burgesses and was one of Virginia's representatives in the Second Continental Congress at which in 1776 the Declaration of Independence was adopted. He was chosen to be Commander in Chief of the Continental Army, and his leadership proved to be one of the decisive factors in uniting the colonies into one nation. After six years of strenuous fighting, he forced the surrender of the British forces at Yorktown in 1781.

Washington now wished to retire, but in 1787 he was called to preside over the Constitutional Convention which had the task of setting up a new form of government for the nation. By unanimous vote, he was elected the first President of the United States in 1789, and was re-elected in 1792. An advocate of strong central government, he guided the nation courageously and successfully through its first critical years. Washington refused a third term and in 1797 retired to Mount Vernon, where he died two years later.

Washington was the only President who did not live in the White House, as he died before it was ready. New York and then Philadelphia were the national capitals during his two terms.

PUBLIC CAREER

Major and Colonel of Virginia Militia; member of Virginia House of Burgesses; delegate to Continental Congress; Commander in Chief of Continental Army; President of Constitutional Convention; Président of the United States.

ADMINISTRATION EVENTS

1789 First Cabinet established
1790 First meeting of Supreme Court
First census taken
Site on Potomac selected for national capital
1791 First ten Amendments (Bill of Rights) adopted
Vermont admitted to Union
First Bank of U. S. chartered by Congress
1792 National Mint established
Kentucky admitted to Union
1794 Federal authority challenged by Whiskey Rebellion
1796 Tennessee admitted to Union

BORN: June 21, 1731
BIRTHPLACE: New Kent County, Virginia
PARENTS: John and Frances Jones Dandridge
MARRIED: Daniel Parke Custis, 1750
  George Washington, 1759
CHILDREN: Four (Custis)
DIED: May 22, 1802. Age, 70

Martha Washington

Maiden Name : Martha Dandridge

LIKE George Washington, Martha was a Virginian; she was born in New Kent County in 1731. She was the daughter of a well-to-do planter, Col. John Dandridge, and grew up on a plantation on the Pamunkey River. Like all girls of Colonial days, she learned to spin, weave, sew, and cook, and she also studied embroidery, dancing, and music. Even as a young girl Martha was noted for her charm and beauty, and when she was 18 years old, she married Col. Daniel Parke Custis, a wealthy planter. But in 1757 Col. Custis died, leaving her a widow with two children. (Two other children had died in infancy.) A year later Martha Custis met young Col. George Washington, and they fell in love at first sight. They were married in January, 1759, and settled down at Mount Vernon.

Their married life was one of mutual love, respect, and admiration that grew stronger with the years. When Washington became Commander in Chief of the Continental Army, Martha shared many of his hardships throughout the war, traveling from camp to camp to care for him, nursing the wounded and sick soldiers and doing her utmost to give them hope and comfort. She was with Washington during the bitter winter at Valley Forge, and she said later that she had heard the first and final shot of practically every important battle.

At the close of the war George and Martha returned to Mount Vernon, but were soon called on to leave it again when Washington was chosen President. In New York, and later in Philadelphia, Martha Washington played her part as the nation's First Lady with a charm and gracious dignity that set a high standard for others to follow. But after Washington's second term ended she was happy to return to the quiet of Mount Vernon. Here, two years later, George died, and Martha survived him by only three and a half years.

Martha and George Washington had no children of their own, but Washington always acted as a father to the two Custis children, John and Martha. When John died during the Revolution, Washington at once adopted two of his children.

*All men are born free and equal,
and have certain natural, essential, and
unalienable rights.*

—CONSTITUTION OF MASSACHUSETTS

John Adams

2nd President, 1797–1801 — Party: Federalist

BORN: October 30, 1735
BIRTHPLACE: Braintree, Massachusetts
PARENTS: John and Susanna Boylston Adams
EDUCATION: Harvard College
RELIGION: Unitarian

OCCUPATION: Lawyer
MARRIED: Abigail Smith, 1764
AGE AT INAUGURATION: 61
TERMS OF OFFICE: One (4 years)
DIED: July 4, 1826. Age, 90

JOHN ADAMS, who had been Vice President during Washington's administrations, succeeded him in 1797 to be the second President of the United States. Adams was one of the outstanding patriots of the Revolution and a "founding father" of the Republic. Born in Massachusetts, he had graduated from Harvard College and had then studied law. Always keenly interested in public affairs, he was one of the first to advocate separation from England. Adams was a Massachusetts delegate to the First Continental Congress (1774), and as a member of the Second Continental Congress helped to draft the Declaration of Independence. He acted as American Commissioner to France during the Revolution, and with Benjamin Franklin and John Jay he negotiated the peace treaty with Great Britain. Later he was the first American Minister to the Court of George III.

Unfortunately, in spite of his undoubted patriotism, his courage, honesty, and integrity, Adams was an unpopular and unhappy President. Proud and stubborn, he resented the influence of Alexander Hamilton in his Cabinet, and the two men became bitter political enemies. His support of the unpopular Alien and Sedition Acts was widely denounced as curtailing freedom of speech and of the press, and one of his most important acts, the peaceful settlement of an undeclared naval war with France, actually brought about his defeat for re-election in 1800. He quarreled with Thomas Jefferson, his Vice President, although in later years they became friends again. His old age was embittered by the feeling that the country he had served so devotedly did not appreciate him.

Adams, however, had the satisfaction of living to see his son, John Quincy Adams, elected President. He died in 1826 on the 50th anniversary of the adoption of the Declaration of Independence. Thomas Jefferson, his comrade of Revolutionary days, died the same day.

PUBLIC CAREER

Member of First Continental Congress; member of Second Continental Congress; U.S. Commissioner to France; U.S. Minister to Holland; U.S. Minister to England; Vice President; President.

ADMINISTRATION EVENTS

1798 Department of the Navy established
Eleventh Amendment adopted
Alien and Sedition Acts passed

1800 White House became official home of President
Library of Congress established

1801 John Marshall appointed Chief Justice of Supreme Court

BORN: November 23, 1744
BIRTHPLACE: Weymouth, Massachusetts
PARENTS: William and Elizabeth Quincy Smith
MARRIED: John Adams, 1764
CHILDREN: 3 sons; 2 daughters
DIED: October 28, 1818. Age, 73

Abigail Adams

Maiden Name : Abigail Smith

ABIGAIL ADAMS was the only First Lady to be both the wife and the mother of a President. Although not a beauty, she was always noted for her keen intelligence, wit, and good judgment and was one of the most distinguished women of her day. She was born and grew up in Massachusetts, the daughter of a Congregational minister, and because of poor health as a child was not sent to school. But her father encouraged her to read in his library, and in this way she acquired an unusually good education.

In Boston she met the rising young lawyer John Adams, and they were married on October 25, 1764. Five children were born to them during the next ten years. In 1774, when Adams was sent to Philadelphia as a delegate to the Continental Congress, Abigail settled down on their farm at Braintree. There she remained during the years of the Revolution, managing the farm, bringing up the children, and sewing and knitting for the soldiers.

Adams' mission to France prolonged their separation, and it was not until 1784 that she was able to join him in Paris. When he was appointed Minister to England the next year, Abigail's tact, good judgment, and friendly spirit played an important part in aiding the diplomatic work of her husband in this difficult post.

Her experience in the courts of France and England made Abigail Adams well qualified for her position as First Lady when her husband became President. Adams frequently discussed his problems with her, and her quick wit and clear thinking often helped him in making important decisions. She was undoubtedly one of

the most influential of all our First Ladies

In November of 1800 President Adams and Abigail moved into the unfinished White House, although the surrounding country was almost a wilderness. Abigail wrote her friends that they could hardly get enough wood for fires, and she used the audience chamber as a drying room for her laundry.

After the end of Adams' term of office, they moved back to the family farm at Braintree, and here Abigail spent her last years. She lived to see her son, John Quincy Adams, become Secretary of State, but died before he became President.

*The cement of this Union
is the heart-blood of every American.*
—WRITINGS, VOLUME XIV

Thomas Jefferson

3rd President, 1801–1809 — Party: Democratic Republican

BORN: April 13, 1743
BIRTHPLACE: Shadwell, Virginia
PARENTS: Peter and Jane Randolph Jefferson
EDUCATION: College of William and Mary
RELIGION: Deist (not a church member)

OCCUPATIONS: Planter and lawyer
MARRIED: Martha Wayles Skelton, 1772
AGE AT INAUGURATION: 57
TERMS OF OFFICE: Two (8 years)
DIED: July 4, 1826. Age, 83

EVEN if Thomas Jefferson had never been elected President, he would still hold an honored place in American history as the author of the Declaration of Independence. Like Washington, he was the son of a Virginia planter of moderate means. After graduating from William and Mary College in Williamsburg, he turned to the law as his profession and distinguished himself as a lawyer, scholar, and statesman. He had a brilliant and lively mind, and was strongly liberal and democratic in his sympathies. He believed in equal rights for all, and supported freedom of religion and of the press.

Like Washington and Adams, he was a delegate to the Second Continental Congress, and because of his literary ability he was selected to write the text of the Declaration of Independence. During the years of the Revolution, Jefferson was Governor of Virginia and took no active part in the fighting. After the close of the war he was sent as American Minister to the Court of France, and returned in 1789 to become Secretary of State in Washington's Cabinet and later Vice President under Adams. Here he found himself opposed to Hamilton, and the two men became leaders of the first political parties in the United States—the Federalists (Hamilton), and the Democratic Republicans (Jefferson).

Elected to succeed John Adams in 1800, Jefferson carried his democratic principles into the White House, putting aside ceremonials and living very simply. During his Presidency he brought about the Louisiana Purchase from France; encouraged the Lewis and Clark Expedition; established West Point Military Academy; and kept the country out of the Napoleonic wars. The Embargo Act, which he forced through Congress to close American markets to France and England, proved unworkable and had to be repealed. Even after his term of office was over he remained the leader of his party. He died on the same day as John Adams—July 4, 1826.

PUBLIC CAREER

Member of Virginia House of Burgesses; member of Second Continental Congress; Governor of Virginia; Minister to France; Secretary of State; Vice President; President.

ADMINISTRATION EVENTS

1801 War with Barbary pirates
1802 West Point Military Academy established
Ohio admitted to Union
1803 Louisiana Territory purchased from France
1804 Twelfth Amendment adopted
1805 Lewis and Clark reached Pacific
1807 Embargo Act passed
Aaron Burr tried for conspiracy

Martha Jefferson Randolph (*daughter*)

BORN: October 19, 1748
BIRTHPLACE: Charles City County, Virginia
PARENTS: John and Martha Eppes Wayles
MARRIED: Bathurst Skelton, 1765
Thomas Jefferson, 1772
CHILDREN: Six (Jefferson). 1 son; 5 daughters
DIED: September 6, 1782. Age, 33

Martha Jefferson

Maiden Name : Martha Wayles

THE wife of Thomas Jefferson was another Martha who also came from Virginia; but unlike Martha Washington, she did not live to become a First Lady. She was born in 1748, the daughter of a wealthy Virginia lawyer, and received an unusually good education. Although no portrait of her exists, she is described as a slenderly beautiful girl with auburn hair and hazel eyes.

At seventeen she married Bathurst Skelton, but within two years he died, and her infant son died, too. Two or three years later she met Thomas Jefferson. They were attracted to each other by their mutual love of music, for Martha was an accomplished musician and Jefferson played the violin.

They were married in January of 1772 on her father's plantation, and then went to live at Jefferson's beautiful estate of Monticello. Jefferson adored his lovely young wife, and she was devoted to him. She admired his intellectual brilliance and his high ideals, and was proud and happy when he was called upon to draft the text for the Declaration of Independence.

Unfortunately, Martha's health was poor and she was a semi-invalid most of their married life. It was largely because of his concern for her and his wish to remain near her that Jefferson did not take a more active part in public affairs during the Revolution. In 1782 her strength failed, and she died on Sept. 6 at the early age of 33.

Jefferson never married again, and when he entered public life his daughter Martha acted as his official hostess. During his terms as President, Dolley Madison, wife of his Secretary of State, often filled these White House duties when his daughter could not be there. Jefferson outlived Martha by 44 years, but he never forgot her. After his death, mementos of her were found in a secret drawer of one of his cabinets.

Six children—a boy and five girls—were born to Martha and Thomas Jefferson, but only two lived to grow up.

The advice nearest to my heart and deepest in my conviction is, that the Union of the states must be cherished and perpetuated.

—ADVICE TO MY COUNTRY

James Madison

4th President, 1809–1817 — Party: Democratic Republican

BORN: March 16, 1751
BIRTHPLACE: Port Conway, Virginia
PARENTS: James and Nelly Conway Madison
EDUCATION: Princeton College
RELIGION: Episcopalian

OCCUPATIONS: Planter; lawyer
MARRIED: Dolley Payne Todd, 1794
AGE AT INAUGURATION: 57
TERMS OF OFFICE: Two (8 years)
DIED: June 28, 1836. Age, 85

SCHOLARLY James Madison was born with a genius for politics. The son of a Virginia planter, he was physically thin and frail, but had a zest for study and excelled in history and government. He attended Princeton College and later studied law under Jefferson, whose plantation was not far from his own home.

Unfit for military service in the Revolution, Madison turned his efforts to the problems of government. He took an active interest in the rights of the colonies from the time of the Stamp Act, was a member of the Continental Congress, and later of the Constitutional Convention of 1787. Because of the ideas he contributed and the large amount of work he did in drafting the original articles and the first ten Amendments, he became known as "the father of the Constitution." Like Jefferson, whom he greatly admired, he believed in the principles of liberty and democracy, favored universal suffrage, states' rights, and decentralization of the government. During Washington's administration he was a member of the House of Representatives, and he served in Jefferson's Cabinet as Secretary of State.

Madison was elected to the Presidency in 1808, succeeding Jefferson, and held office for eight troubled years. Although a peace-loving man, he was reluctantly obliged to declare war on England in 1812 to establish the commercial rights of the United States on the high seas. The war, unpopular with the public, was called "Mr. Madison's War," and at one time when the British captured and burned Washington, President Madison was obliged to flee from his capital. However, the war ended victoriously for the United States and an era of national expansion began.

At the close of his term, Madison retired to his estate of Montpelier in Virginia, but he continued to take an active interest in public affairs, and joined with Jefferson in founding the University of Virginia. He was 85 when he died in 1836.

PUBLIC CAREER

Member of Virginia legislature; member of Continental Congress; member of Constitutional Convention; member of House of Representatives; Secretary of State; President.

ADMINISTRATION EVENTS

1812 War declared against Great Britain
Louisiana admitted to the Union

1814 Washington burned by the British
Francis Scott Key wrote "The Star Spangled Banner"

1815 Battle of New Orleans

1816 Indiana admitted to Union

BIRTHDAY: May 20, 1768
BIRTHPLACE: Guilford County, North Carolina
PARENTS: John and Mary Coles Payne
MARRIED: John Todd, 1790
James Madison, 1794
CHILDREN: 2 sons (Todd)
DIED: July 12, 1849. Age, 81

Dolley Madison

Maiden Name : Dolley Payne

DOLLEY MADISON, wife of our fourth President is known as the gayest and perhaps the most glamorous of all our First Ladies. She was born in North Carolina, the daughter of Quaker parents. In 1783, her parents moved to Philadelphia, and there she met and married her first husband, John Todd, a lawyer. He died during a yellow fever epidemic, leaving her a widow with one child. An earlier baby had died.

Aaron Burr, a friend of the family, introduced the beautiful young Quaker widow to James Madison, then a member of Congress from Virginia. In spite of the difference of 17 years in their ages, they were attracted to each other and were married in September of 1794. Since Madison was a Episcopalian, Dolley was "read out" of her own church, and joined his.

Dolley now entered upon a life much more to her liking than the sober Quaker style. She quickly became a famous hostess and social leader in Philadelphia and later in Washington. Her beauty, friendliness, warm personality, gay spirits, and tactfulness not only won her a host of personal friends, but were also a great political asset to her husband. Madison was a plain, serious-minded man lacking in personal charm, and it was often due to Dolley that he was able to win the support of important politicians.

When Madison became President in 1809, one of Dolley's first projects was to redecorate the White House, and the inauguration ball was a dazzling affair. Then in 1814, when the British burned Washington, it was Dolley who saved the portrait of George Washington and many of Madison's important state papers, carrying them away in her carriage as she fled the city in disguise. It was Dolley, too, who persuaded Madison that he must rebuild the capital.

At the close of Madison's term as President, they returned to his estate of Montpelier in Virginia, where Dolley devoted herself largely to caring for her husband until his death in 1836. She then moved to Washington, where she was a distinguished figure in society until her death in 1849.

The Madisons had no children. Dolley's one son, named Payne Todd, was the child of her first marriage.

The American Continents are henceforth not to be considered as subjects for future colonization by any European powers.

—MESSAGE TO CONGRESS, 1823

James Monroe

5th President, 1817–1825 — Party: Democratic Republican

BORN: April 28, 1758
BIRTHPLACE: Westmoreland County, Virginia
PARENTS: Spence and Elizabeth Jones Monroe
EDUCATION: College of William and Mary
RELIGION: Episcopalian

OCCUPATIONS: Planter; lawyer
MARRIED: Elizabeth Kortright, 1786
AGE AT INAUGURATION: 58
TERMS OF OFFICE: Two (8 years)
DIED: July 4, 1831. Age, 73

PRESIDENT MONROE gave his name to one of our nation's most significant documents: the Monroe Doctrine. This doctrine, stating as its two main principles that (1) the American continents were no longer open to colonization and (2) that there must be no European interference with American nations, has ever since been one of the cornerstones of American foreign policy.

James Monroe, like Washington, Jefferson, and Madison, was a Virginian. He attended the College of William and Mary, but left his studies in 1776 to fight in the War for Independence under Washington. After the war he studied law under Thomas Jefferson, and then began his career of public service. He served in his state legislature, in the Continental Congress, and in the U. S. Senate. He was sent as an envoy to France by Washington and again by Jefferson, and helped negotiate the treaty for the purchase of the Louisiana Territory. He served 4 terms as Governor of Virginia, and as Secretary of War and of State under Madison he carried on the war against England with courage and vigor.

His two terms as President, succeeding Madison, were known as the "era of good feeling"— a period of political peace both abroad and at home. Monroe surrounded himself with capable men and his administration was marked by notable achievements in foreign affairs, in commerce, and in western development. His statement of the Monroe Doctrine checked European colonization in South America; he negotiated an agreement with England pledging both nations to disarm on the Great Lakes; and he bought Florida from Spain. The Missouri Compromise, limiting the westward expansion of slavery, also was passed during his administration.

Monroe lived only six years after his retirement. He died on July 4, 1831, in New York City.

PUBLIC CAREER

Captain and Major in Continental Army; member of Virginia legislature; member of Continental Congress; U.S. Senator; Minister to France; Spain; England; Governor of Virginia; Secretary of War and of State, President.

ADMINISTRATION EVENTS

1817 Mississippi admitted to Union
1818 Illinois admitted to Union
1819 Alabama admitted to Union
Florida purchased from Spain
1820 Maine admitted to Union
Missouri Compromise enacted
1821 Missouri admitted to Union
1823 The Monroe Doctrine proclaimed

BORN: June 30, 1768
BIRTHPLACE: New York City
PARENTS: Captain Lawrence
   and Hannah Aspinwall Kortright
MARRIED: James Monroe, 1786
CHILDREN: 2 daughters, 1 son
DIED: September 23, 1830. Age, 62

Elizabeth Monroe

Maiden Name : Elizabeth Kortright

THE BELLE of New York" was the title given to the beautiful and aristocratic Elizabeth Kortright when she was a girl in New York City. Born in 1768, she was the daughter of a retired officer of the British Army, Capt. Lawrence Kortright, who became a loyal American after the Revolution. Her mother was a member of a prominent Colonial family, and Elizabeth grew up accustomed to New York society.

Elizabeth met James Monroe when he came to New York as one of the younger members of the Continental Congress from Virginia. They were married in 1786, when she was 18 years old and Monroe ten years older. They first made their home in Fredericksburg, Va., where the first of their two daughters was born. When Monroe was appointed U.S. Minister to France in 1794, Elizabeth accompanied him and made many friends there. The French Revolution was then going on, and Elizabeth Monroe, through her influence, helped to save the life of Madame Lafayette, who had been condemned to death as an aristocrat.

Monroe was later sent to Paris again by Jefferson to help negotiate the terms of the Louisiana Purchase, and after this to London. Elizabeth was unhappy in the unfriendly atmosphere of the British Court and suffered much from the cold, damp climate. They returned to the U.S. in 1807.

When Monroe was elected to succeed Madison as President in 1816, Elizabeth Monroe proved herself well qualified for the duties of First Lady. Her experience in the courts of Europe as well as her own upbringing fitted her for social leadership in the capital. Also, she was devoted to her husband and proud to aid him in any way she could. Her insistence on a certain formality in social procedure made her unpopular with some of the society matrons, but they could not help being impressed with her elegance and good taste. One of her important achievements was the redecoration of the White House, which had been burned during the War of 1812. Increasing ill health, however, forced her to give up much of her social activities. Her second daughter was married in the White House in 1820.

After the close of Monroe's second term, in 1825, they retired at last to their Virginia estate of Oak Hill, and here Elizabeth died, on Sept. 23, 1830.

*Our Constitution professedly rests
upon the good sense and attachment
of the people. This basis, weak as it may appear,
has not yet been found to fail.*

—LETTERS (1801)

John Quincy Adams

6th President, 1825–1829 — Party: Democratic Republican

BORN: July 11, 1767
BIRTHPLACE: Braintree, Massachusetts
PARENTS: John and Abigail Smith Adams
EDUCATION: Harvard College
RELIGION: Unitarian

OCCUPATION: Lawyer
MARRIED: Louisa Catherine Johnson, 1797
AGE AT INAUGURATION: 57
TERMS OF OFFICE: one (4 years)
DIED: February 23, 1848. Age, 80

JOHN QUINCY ADAMS, son of our second President, had one of the longest careers of public service in our history. At the age of 14 he was secretary to the American Minister to Russia; at the age of 80, when he died, he was a member of Congress.

Adams was born in Braintree, Mass., and when only seven years old watched the Battle of Bunker Hill with his mother, Abigail Adams. When he was ten, his father, John Adams, took him abroad on his diplomatic travels, and four years later he went to St. Petersburg as secretary to the legation there. Later he lived with his father in Holland and in London, but he returned to the United States to attend Harvard College and then took up the study of law. He was elected to the Massachusetts Senate in 1802, and then to the U. S. Senate. From 1809–14 he was U. S. Minister to Russia, and was then appointed to the commission which negotiated the terms of peace ending the War of 1812. As Secretary of State under President Monroe, he helped to draft the Monroe Doctrine.

By 1824 the old Federalist party had died out and all the candidates for Presidency were nominally Democratic Republicans. John Quincy Adams and Andrew Jackson were the leading candidates. Jackson won the most popular votes,

but because he did not have a majority of the electoral votes the election was decided by the House of Representatives, who chose Adams.

Like his father, John Quincy Adams was a man of high integrity and courage, but like him, too, he was stubborn and uncompromising. He supported the doctrine of high tariffs, believed in a strongly centralized government, encouraged internal improvements, and took a strong stand against slavery. Adams' followers became known as the National Republican Party, as opposed to Jackson's Democrats.

Adams was defeated for re-election, but his usefulness was by no means over. Two years later he was elected to the House of Representatives as a member from Massachusetts. He served in Congress until fatally stricken with paralysis on the floor of the House on Feb. 23, 1848.

PUBLIC CAREER

Minister to Holland; Minister to Portugal; Minister to Prussia; Massachusetts state senator; U. S. Senator; Minister to Russia; Peace Commissioner at Ghent; Minister to England; Secretary of State; President.

ADMINISTRATION EVENTS

1825 Erie Canal completed
1828 "Tariff of Abominations" passed

BORN: February 12, 1775
BIRTHPLACE: London, England
PARENTS: Joshua and Catherine Nuth Johnson
MARRIED: John Quincy Adams, 1797
CHILDREN: 3 sons; 1 daughter
DIED: May 14, 1852. Age, 77

Louisa Adams

Maiden Name : Louisa Catherine Johnson

LOUISA JOHNSON Adams was our only First Lady of foreign birth. Her father, Joshua Johnson, was an American living in England for business reasons, and her mother was an Englishwoman. Louisa was born in 1775, just before the outbreak of the Revolution, and two years later her father moved to France so that he could work openly for the colonists. After the war he returned to London as American consul, and here, in 1795, the 20-year-old Louisa met young John Quincy Adams, already an experienced diplomat. She was attracted to the brilliant young man, and he was equally charmed by her beauty and accomplishments. They were married in 1797 and shortly afterward Adams was appointed Minister to Prussia, so that Louisa did not see the United States until 1801.

After several years in Washington, Adams was appointed American Minister to Russia, and here Louisa spent five cold and lonely years. Probably the most exciting adventure of her life was when she had to journey by coach all the way from St. Petersburg to Paris in midwinter to join her husband, who was carrying on negotiations following the close of the War of 1812. This would have been a hazardous trip even for a man in war-torn Europe, yet Louisa accomplished it successfully, accompanied only by her seven-year-old son. Then, after two years in London, they at last returned to the United States, where Adams was appointed Secretary of State under President Monroe.

Mrs. Adams soon became a popular and gracious leader of Washington society, a position she retained after Adams was elected President in 1824 and she became First Lady. A ball she gave for General Jackson was celebrated in newspaper verse as follows:

Wend you with the World tonight?
 Brown and fair, and wise and witty,
Eyes that float in seas of light,
 Laughing mouths and dimples pretty,
Belles and matrons, maids and madams,
 Are all gone to Mrs. Adams'.

Even after Adams' defeat for a second term they continued to live in Washington, where Adams served in Congress for many years. Louisa survived her husband by four years, dying in the spring of 1852.

Our Federal Union—
it must and shall be preserved.
—TOAST, APRIL 30, 1830

Andrew Jackson

7th President, 1829–1837 — Party: Democratic

BORN: March 15, 1767
BIRTHPLACE: Waxhaw settlement, Carolina border
PARENTS: Andrew and Elizabeth Hutchinson Jackson
RELIGION: Presbyterian
EDUCATION: No formal schooling

OCCUPATIONS: Soldier; lawyer
MARRIED: Rachel Donelson Robards, 1791
AGE AT INAUGURATION: 61
TERMS OF OFFICE: Two (8 years)
DIED: June 8, 1845. Age, 78

ANDREW JACKSON was our first "log cabin" President. The son of poor Scotch-Irish immigrant parents, he grew up in the rough backwoods of the Carolina frontier, and was left an orphan at 15. Already at that early age he had fought against the British in the Revolutionary War and had almost died in a prison camp.

Ambitious to improve himself, he studied law and moved to a settlement near Nashville, Tenn., where he later became a judge. He also served briefly in the U. S. Congress, and when the War of 1812 brought an outbreak of Indian raids, Jackson was chosen to lead an expedition against the Indians of Alabama. His victories over the Indians there, and later over the British forces in Mobile, and finally his victory in the Battle of New Orleans, made him a national hero. His soldiers gave him the nickname of "Old Hickory" because of his toughness. President Monroe appointed Jackson Governor of Florida in 1821, and he was elected to the U. S. Senate in 1822. Although he lost the election for the Presidency in 1824, he ran again in 1828 and won a sweeping victory over Adams. The frontiersmen and the common people regarded Jackson as one of themselves; they admired his fiery temper, his independent spirit, and his democratic manners.

As President, Jackson killed the bill for rechartering the Bank of the United States, which had originally been set up by Alexander Hamilton. He also forced South Carolina to recall its "act of nullification" regarding Federal tariffs, compelled France to pay claims for her attacks on United States commerce during the War of 1812, and paid off the national debt. But he also inaugurated the "spoils system" by freely rewarding his friends and supporters with political offices.

After retiring from office, Jackson returned to his home, The Hermitage, near Nashville, where he died in 1845.

PUBLIC CAREER

U. S. Congressman; Judge, Supreme Court of Tennessee; Major General, Tennessee militia; Major General, U. S. Army; Governor of Florida; U. S. Senator; President.

ADMINISTRATION EVENTS

1829 Postmaster General becomes Cabinet Member
1830 Webster-Hayne debates on states' rights
1832 Bill to recharter Bank of U. S. vetoed
Black Hawk War
1834 McCormick reaper patented
1836 Arkansas admitted to Union
Battle of the Alamo
1837 Michigan admitted to Union

BORN: June 15, 1767
BIRTHPLACE: Halifax County, Virginia
PARENTS: John and Rachel Stockley Donelson
MARRIED: Capt. Lewis Robards, 1785
  Andrew Jackson, 1791
CHILDREN: none
DIED: December 22, 1828. Age, 61 years

Rachel Jackson

Maiden Name : Rachel Donelson

RACHEL DONELSON, the wife of President Jackson, grew up in the frontier settlements of Tennessee and Kentucky. Her father, a Col. John Donelson of Virginia, a member of the House of Burgesses there for three terms, emigrated to Tennessee in 1779, and was one of the founders of the settlement of Nashville. When Rachel was 17, the family moved again, this time to the Kentucky frontier, and here she met and married her first husband, Capt. Lewis Robards. This marriage was brief and unhappy, and she left Robards to return to her mother's home in Nashville.

Rachel met Andrew Jackson, then a young frontier lawyer, and they were at once attracted to each other. She was about 22 years old at this time and a gay, high-spirited girl. In 1791, believing reports they received that Robards had obtained a divorce, Andrew and Rachel were married in Natchez, Miss. For two years they lived together happily; then they learned that Robards had not obtained a divorce in 1791 and that the decree had just become final. Immediately they applied for another license and were remarried, but gossipers never forgot the fact

that for two years their marriage had been illegal. The malicious stories and accusations that were spread about them ruined Rachel's happiness and affected her health, and drove Andrew into duels more than once. They were devoted to each other and Andrew did everything he could to protect Rachel and to show his loyalty to her, but as Jackson advanced in public life, she remained as much as possible at home.

In the years following the War of 1812, when General Jackson was acclaimed as the "Hero of New Orleans," Rachel enjoyed a brief season of popularity and happiness, but when he was nominated for the Presidency the old scandal broke out again more violently than ever. All of Jackson's efforts could not save Rachel from bitter humiliation. She lived to see him elected, but died of a heart attack on Dec. 22, 1828, and was buried at Nashville in the white satin gown designed for the inauguration. Faithful to her memory, Jackson never married again.

Rachel and Andrew Jackson had no children of their own, but they adopted the child of a relative and gave him the name of Andrew Jackson, Jr.

I tread in the footsteps of illustrious men in receiving from the people the sacred trust confided to my illustrious predecessor.

—INAUGURAL ADDRESS, 1837

Martin Van Buren

8th President, 1837–1841 — Party: Democratic

BORN: December 5, 1782
BIRTHPLACE: Kinderhook, New York
PARENTS: Abraham and Mary Hoes Van Buren
EDUCATION: Local schools
RELIGION: Dutch Reformed

OCCUPATION: Lawyer
MARRIED: Hannah Hoes, 1807
AGE AT INAUGURATION: 54
TERMS OF OFFICE: One (4 years)
DIED: July 24, 1862. Age, 79

MARTIN VAN BUREN was the first President from New York State, and also the first one actually born under the American flag. Of Dutch descent, he was born in 1782 and grew up in the little Dutch community of Kinderhook, N. Y., where his father was a farmer and tavern keeper. He began the study of law when 14 years old and was eventually admitted to the bar. He entered politics at an early age also and became an ardent Democrat and supporter of Andrew Jackson. After rising through lower political offices, he became a state senator, then state attorney general, and was elected to the U. S. Senate in 1820. At the time Jackson was elected to the Presidency, Van Buren became Governor of New York, but he resigned this office to become Secretary of State in Jackson's Cabinet. In this position he was influential in shaping national policies, and became noted as a clever political leader.

President Jackson appointed Van Buren the U. S. Minister to England, but the Senate refused to approve the appointment and he had to be recalled. Compensation for this disappointment came when he was elected Vice President for Jackson's second term and practically chosen as his successor.

When Van Buren became President in 1837, he was faced with a financial panic which had struck the country after a period of boom and over-speculation. In dealing with this crisis, Van Buren sponsored the Independent Treasury System, which made the U. S. Treasury independent of the banks. Opposition to his financial policies, as well as labor disturbances and general political unrest, brought about Van Buren's defeat in the elections in 1840. Perhaps because of his rather dandified taste in clothes, his opponents pictured him as a wealthy New York aristocrat who was indifferent to the common people, in contrast to the "log cabin" candidate, William Henry Harrison.

Although he served only one term as President, Van Buren remained active in politics for a number of years before retiring to his estate at Kinderhook, N.Y., where he died in his 79th year.

PUBLIC CAREER

County surrogate; state senator; state attorney-general; U. S. Senator; Governor of New York; Secretary of State; Vice President; President.

ADMINISTRATION EVENTS

1837 Business panic and depression
1838 Boundary treaty with Texas signed
1840 National Treasury established

BORN: March 8, 1783
BIRTHPLACE: Kinderhook, New York
MARRIED: Martin Van Buren, 1807
CHILDREN: 4 sons
DIED: February 5, 1819. Age, 35

Hannah Van Buren

Maiden Name : Hannah Hoes

HANNAH HOES and Martin Van Buren were distant cousins and grew up together in the little Dutch community of Kinderhook, N. Y. Born in 1783, she was only one year younger than Martin and they were classmates at school. As they grew up, they shared each other's interests more and more, and after Martin finished his law studies they soon became engaged.

Hannah and Martin were married on Feb. 21, 1807, and a year or so later moved to Hudson, N. Y., a busy shipbuilding town, where Martin, now 25 years old, began his career in law and politics. Hannah's first child had been born in Kinderhook; two more were born after the move to Hudson. There are few records of Hannah herself, but an early portrait shows her as dainty and doll-like with blue eyes and light brown hair.

Some nine years later, after being elected to the state senate, Van Buren decided to move to Albany, the state capital. This was an even larger and more impressive city than Hudson, and Hannah was happy to find many Dutch people living there. Hannah was naturally proud of her husband's growing reputation, but city life did not agree with her and after a winter of severe cold her health began to fail. She died in February of 1819, after the birth of her fourth child. She was then only 35 years old. It was not until 18 years later that Martin Van Buren became President, but he never married again, and at White House receptions he received the guests alone. On her gravestone he had the following inscription carved: "She was a sincere Christian, a faithful child, a tender mother, an affectionate wife. Precious shall be the memory of her virtues."

Hannah and Martin had four sons, and after the eldest, Major Abraham Van Buren, was married, he brought his bride, Angelica Singleton Van Buren, to the White House to live. During the troubled years of Martin Van Buren's administration, when he was faced with so many political and financial problems, she took over the duties of White House hostess and fulfilled them with charm and competence.

We admit of no government by divine right;
the only legitimate right to govern
is an express grant of power from the governed.
—INAUGURAL ADDRESS, 1841

William Henry Harrison

9th President, 1841 (1 month) — Party: Whig

BORN: February 9, 1773
BIRTHPLACE: Berkeley, Virginia
PARENTS: Benjamin and Elizabeth Bassett Harrison
EDUCATION: Hampden-Sidney College
RELIGION: Episcopalian

OCCUPATION: Soldier
MARRIED: Anna Symmes, 1795
AGE AT INAUGURATION: 68
TERM OF OFFICE: 1 month
DIED: April 4, 1841. Age, 68

ALTHOUGH William Henry Harrison is usually thought of as a frontiersman and Indian fighter, he was actually the son of one of Virginia's leading colonial families and was educated at Hampden-Sidney College. His father, who was one of the signers of the Declaration of Independence, wanted his son to become a doctor, and he accordingly attended a medical school in Philadelphia for a time. On his father's death, however, Harrison left school to join the fight against the Indians who were menacing the white settlers in the old Northwest Territory. He served for a time under "Mad Anthony" Wayne, acquired a reputation for good judgment and honesty, and when the Territory of Indiana was formed in 1800, he was appointed governor. He won an increased reputation for his victories over the Indian chief Tecumseh, especially at the Battle of Tippecanoe, in Indiana. In the War of 1812 he was commissioned a major general and led his forces into Canada to defeat the British at the Battle of the Thames.

After the close of the war, Harrison retired from the army and was elected to terms in both the House of Representatives and the Senate. He was appointed U. S. Minister to Colombia, but was recalled by President Jackson, and then settled down on his farm in Ohio. In 1840 the

Whigs, looking for a candidate to oppose Van Buren, chose Harrison, "the hero of Tippecanoe," as a representative of the western frontier. His political opponents sneered at him for his "log cabin" background, and the log cabin henceforth became his symbol. To the general public he was a much more colorful and appealing figure than the New York lawyer Van Buren, and he was elected. His running mate for Vice President was John Tyler of Virginia.

Unfortunately President Harrison caught a cold during the inauguration ceremonies on March 4, 1841, and died of pneumonia a month later, at the age of 68. He was buried at North Bend, Ohio.

Aside from his election to the Presidency, William Henry Harrison is remembered chiefly for his work as Governor of Indiana Territory during its first years. He was also the oldest man ever elected to the Presidency.

PUBLIC CAREER

Army captain; Secretary of Northwest Territory; Territorial delegate; Governor of Territory of Indiana; Major General, U. S. Army; member of Congress; state senator; U. S. Senator; U. S. Minister to Colombia; President.

BORN: July 25, 1775
BIRTHPLACE: Morristown, New Jersey
PARENTS: John and Susan Livingston Symmes
MARRIED: William Henry Harrison, 1795
CHILDREN: 6 sons; 4 daughters
DIED: February 25, 1864. Age, 89

Anna Harrison

Maiden Name : Anna Symmes

ANNA HARRISON was a First Lady for a shorter period than any other President's wife, yet she lived longer than any other First Lady, to date. Born during the first year of the Revolutionary War (1775), she lived almost to the end of the Civil War, dying in 1864.

Anna was the daughter of John Symmes, a judge, and she was born in Morristown, N. J. Since her mother died shortly after her birth, and her father was then an officer in the Continental Army, she was brought up by her grandparents on Long Island, N. Y.

Judge Symmes became interested in the possibilities of the wild land north of the Ohio River, and when the Northwest Territory was organized, he acquired a large tract of land there. In 1787 he was appointed a Supreme Court Justice in Cincinnati, and in 1794 he brought Anna there, together with his second wife, to live in a new home at North Bend, Ohio.

Life in the crude little frontier settlement was far different from what Anna had known in New York, but it was here she met her future husband. William Henry Harrison was at that time 22 years old, and an aide to "Mad Anthony" Wayne. Anna and William were married in 1795, in spite of her father's objections, who doubted Harrison's ability to support his daughter.

From now on, Anna lived the greater part of her life on the western frontier. After Harrison was appointed Governor of the Indiana Territory in 1800, he built a brick home on land north of Vincennes, and this was their home for 12 years. Often during this period Anna had to manage the plantation alone, while Harrison was away on official business. When the War of 1812 broke out, Anna returned to her father's home in Cincinnati. After the war Harrison later joined her here, and the farm at North Bend became their home. Ten children were born to them, although five died.

When Harrison suddenly became a candidate for the Presidency in 1840, Anna was 65 years old and was unable to accompany her husband to his inauguration because of poor health. She received word of his sudden death a month later, just as she was preparing to join him.

After the President's death, Mrs. Harrison continued to live at North Bend with her son, John Scott Harrison, who was the father of Benjamin Harrison, later to become the 23rd President. Anna, however, did not live to see her grandson in the White House. She died in 1864 at the age of 89 years.

So far as it depends on the course of this government, our relations of good will and friendship will be sedulously cultivated with all nations.

—MESSAGE TO CONGRESS, 1841

John Tyler

10th President, 1841–1845 — Party: Whig

BORN: March 29, 1790

BIRTHPLACE: Greenway, Virginia

PARENTS: John and Mary Armistead Tyler

EDUCATION: College of William and Mary

RELIGION: Episcopalian

OCCUPATION: Lawyer

MARRIED: Letitia Christian, 1813
Julia Gardiner, 1844

AGE AT INAUGURATION: 51

TERMS OF OFFICE: One (less 1 month)

DIED: January 18, 1862. Age, 71

JOHN TYLER, who succeeded Harrison to the Presidency, was the first Vice President to fill the unexpired term of a President. He was a Virginian by birth, a graduate of William and Mary College, and a lawyer by profession. Before becoming Vice President, he had served in the Virginia legislature, had been both a U. S. Representative and Senator, and had been Governor of Virginia for one term.

Tyler was a man of independent views and cared little for party loyalty. Although a Democrat during Jackson's administration, he disagreed with Jackson's policy in dealing with the Bank of the United States, and as a Southerner, he opposed Jackson on the issue of "states' rights." In 1840 the Whigs chose him as their candidate for Vice President to secure Southern votes, using the slogan: "Tippecanoe and Tyler too."

When Harrison died one month after his inauguration, Tyler, in accordance with the Constitution, succeeded to the Presidency. But although now the head of the Whig party, he refused to support many of their platform principles. He believed in "strict construction" of the Constitution, and when Congress passed a bill to reincorporate the Bank of the United States, Tyler twice vetoed it. The angry Whigs read him out of their party, and all of his Cabinet, except

Daniel Webster, resigned. He then formed a Democratic Cabinet, but for the rest of his term he was on such bad terms with Congress and so unpopular with the public that little of importance was accomplished during his administration.

Neither the Whigs nor the Democrats offered to support Tyler for re-election, and he accordingly retired to private life after his one term of office. He never held any other important political office, but in 1861 he came to Washington as president of the Peace Convention that sought unsuccessfully to avert the Civil War. After Virginia voted to secede, he was elected to the Confederate Congress, but died before taking office. He was buried in Richmond.

PUBLIC CAREER

Member of Virginia legislature; U. S. Representative; Governor of Virginia; U.S. Senator; Vice President; President.

ADMINISTRATION EVENTS

1841 Independent Treasury Act repealed

1842 Ashburton Treaty, fixing boundaries of Maine and Canada, signed

1844 Treaty opening China to American trade signed

1845 Bill for annexation of Texas signed
Florida admitted to the Union

Letitia Tyler

Maiden Name : Letitia Christian

BORN: November 12, 1790
BIRTHPLACE: New Kent County, Virginia
PARENTS: Robert and Mary Brown Christian
MARRIED: John Tyler, 1813
CHILDREN: 3 sons, 5 daughters
DIED: September 10, 1842. Age, 51

LETITIA CHRISTIAN, who became President Tyler's first wife, was born near Richmond, Virginia. Her father was a well-to-do planter, and Letitia is described as an aristocratic beauty. She became engaged to John Tyler, son of the Governor of Virginia, when they were both 18 years old, but it was five years before her parents would consent to the marriage.

The young couple first lived on a modest farm, but after the death of Tyler's parents, he inherited the family plantation. Letitia, quiet and domestic by nature, proved a good manager, and she took over most of the care of family affairs.

Tyler, elected Vice President in 1840, became President after Harrison's death in 1841. Letitia, however, was scarcely able to take on the duties of First Lady. She had suffered a stroke in 1838 and had been an invalid ever since. Almost her only social appearance at the White House was at the marriage of her daughter Elizabeth in January, 1842, and a few months later, in September, she died.

Julia Tyler

Maiden Name : Julia Gardiner

BORN: May 4, 1820
BIRTHPLACE: New York, New York
PARENTS: David and Juliana McLachlen Gardiner
MARRIED: John Tyler, 1844
CHILDREN: 5 sons, 2 daughters
DIED: July 10, 1889. Age, 69

PRESIDENT Tyler's second wife was Julia Gardiner, a beautiful girl belonging to one of New York's oldest families, and called by her admirers "the Rose of Long Island."

Julia met President Tyler at a White House dinner early in 1844, and he was immediately attracted to her. This feeling was doubtless increased by the tragic accident which resulted in her father's death when he and Julia were guests on the President's flagship a short time later. In June of 1844 they were quietly married in New York, and Julia became the second First Lady.

Julia's youth, gaiety, and social gifts made her a very popular hostess, and in spite of the 30 years difference in their ages, she and John Tyler apparently lived very happily together. After his term of office was over, they returned to his estate in Virginia, and when the Civil War broke out, Julia, like her husband, joined the Southern cause. After his death in 1862 she remained in the South and never remarried, although she was a widow for 27 years.

The blessings of Liberty which our Constitution secures may be enjoyed alike by minorities and majorities.

—INAUGURAL ADDRESS

James Knox Polk

11th President, 1845–1849 — Party: Democratic

BORN: November 2, 1795
BIRTHPLACE: Little Sugar Creek, North Carolina
PARENTS: Samuel and Jane Knox Polk
EDUCATION: University of North Carolina
RELIGION: Methodist

OCCUPATION: Lawyer
MARRIED: Sarah Childress, 1824
AGE AT INAUGURATION: 49
TERMS OF OFFICE: One (4 years)
DIED: June 15, 1849. Age, 53

JAMES KNOX POLK was the first "dark horse" candidate to become President. It had been expected that Martin Van Buren would be nominated by the Democratic party in the Convention of 1844, but when he could not win the support of two-thirds of delegates, the convention swung its support to Polk, who had been considered for the Vice Presidency.

James Knox Polk's parents were farmers in North Carolina, but when he was about 10 years old they moved to Tennessee. Polk attended the University of North Carolina and then began to practice law in Tennessee. He was elected to the U. S. Congress and served there for 14 years, making a reputation as a brilliant orator, and eventually becoming Speaker of the House. He then served one term as Governor of Tennessee before becoming the Democratic candidate for the Presidency in 1844.

President Polk is remembered for his firm stand in admitting Texas to the Union and for his resistance to British claims to the Oregon Territory. An act authorizing the annexation of Texas had been signed by Tyler on his last day in office, but the boundary between Texas and Mexico was unsettled. Polk sent troops to the Texas border, and clashes between these troops and the Mexican soldiers led to the War of 1846.

The eventual peace treaty in 1848 added the rich territories of California, New Mexico, and Arizona to the United States. About the same time, the dispute with England over the Oregon boundary was adjusted, and the advance of our western boundaries to the Pacific was accomplished. Discovery of gold in California in 1848 started a great westward rush. Another important act of his administration was the re-establishment of the Independent Treasury System, which had been repealed by the Whigs.

Polk's health failed under the strain of his years as President, and he did not seek renomination. He died only three months after retiring to his home in Nashville, Tenn.

PUBLIC CAREER

Member of Tennessee legislature; member of U.S. Congress; Speaker of the House; Governor of Tennessee; President.

ADMINISTRATION EVENTS

1845 Texas admitted to Union
U.S. Naval Academy established at Annapolis
1846-48 War with Mexico
1846 Oregon boundary question settled
Iowa admitted to Union
1848 Wisconsin admitted to Union
Gold discovered in California

BORN: September 4, 1803
BIRTHPLACE: Murfreesboro, Tennessee
PARENTS: Joel and Elizabeth Childress
MARRIED: James Polk, 1824
CHILDREN: None
DIED: August 14, 1891. Age, 87

Sarah Polk

Maiden Name : Sarah Childress

WHEN James Polk became President in 1845, he brought to the White House a First Lady very different from the gay and fashionable Julia Tyler. Sarah Polk was a woman of serious and intellectual nature. She had been born near Murfreesboro, Tenn., the daughter of a well-to-do merchant, and received a strictly religious education at the Moravian Institute in Salem, N. C.

Andrew Jackson knew both James Polk and Sarah Childress and it has been suggested that he brought them together and advised Polk that Sarah would make him a good wife. At any rate, the two young people were married in 1824 when Sarah was 20 years old. From the first, she shared her husband's ambition for a political career and dedicated her entire life to him. During the years when he was advancing as a state congressman, U. S. Representative, and as Governor of Tennessee, she helped him with his speeches. When he became the "dark horse" Democratic candidate in 1844 she worked with him constantly as his confidential secretary to help win the election.

As First Lady, Sarah Polk presided over the White House with dignity and grace, but her entertainments were mainly in the form of state dinners and receptions or musicals. Because of her strict religious upbringing, she banned alcoholic liquors, card playing, and dancing and took little part in the purely social life of the capital. She continued to act as her husband's confidential secretary all during his term of office—the first and perhaps the only First Lady to play such a part.

Polk's health suffered under the strain of his years as President, and Sarah was glad when they were able to retire to Nashville in 1849. After his death in 1849, Sarah continued to live in Nashville, devoting herself to the management of her business interests. She had no children and she never remarried.

During the Civil War her sympathies were with the Southern people, but at her home in Nashville she entertained the officers of both the Confederate and the Union armies with equal dignity.

Her home in Nashville became a shrine to the memory of her husband, and she preserved there all of his papers and mementoes. She died in 1891, and was buried in Nashville.

*In the discharge of duties my guide will
be the Constitution, which I this day swear
to preserve, protect, and defend.*

—INAUGURAL ADDRESS, 1849

Zachary Taylor

12th President, 1849–1850 — Party: Whig

BORN: November 24, 1784
BIRTHPLACE: Orange County, Virginia
PARENTS: Richard and Sarah Strother Taylor
EDUCATION: Self-taught
RELIGION: Episcopalian

OCCUPATION: Soldier
MARRIED: Margaret Smith, 1810
AGE AT INAUGURATION: 64
TERM OF OFFICE: 16 months
DIED: July 9, 1850. Age, 65

ZACHARY TAYLOR was a second cousin of James Madison, our fourth President. The son of an officer in the Continental Army, he was born in Virginia but grew up in the frontier regions of Kentucky. As a result, he had only a very limited education. The life of a frontier farmer did not appeal to Zachary, and when he was 23 years old he joined the regular army, where his resourcefulness and gallantry in action won him rapid advancement. He took part in campaigns against the Indians in the Old Northwest and in Florida, and served with distinction in the War of 1812. Appointed a major general, he was sent by President Polk to defend the Texas border in 1846, and became a national hero for his defeat of the Mexican forces under Santa Anna at the battle of Buena Vista. His soldiers gave him the affectionate nickname of "Old Rough and Ready."

Because of his popularity as a war hero, the Whig party offered him the nomination as presidential candidate in 1848, and after some hesitation he accepted. He defeated the leading Whig, Henry Clay, for the nomination and was elected over the Democratic candidate, Lewis Cass, by a small majority.

Since General Taylor had never held political office or been active in politics, even his own party did not know how he stood on important national questions, such as slavery. He soon made it clear, however, that although a Southerner and a slave-holder himself, he intended to uphold the Constitution and the Union. When the question came up of whether California was to be admitted as a free state or a slave state, he bluntly rebuked certain hotheads who talked about secession, and warned against the dangers of rebellion. "I will command the army in person and hang any man taken in treason," he threatened.

President Taylor's term was too short to determine what success he might have had as President. On July 4, 1850, while laying the cornerstone of the Washington Monument, he became ill and died five days later.

PUBLIC CAREER

Army officer; Major General; President.

ADMINISTRATION EVENTS

1849 Department of Interior created
California "gold rush" began
1850 Slavery debate in Congress, leading to Compromise of 1850
Overland Mail Service started
Clayton-Bulwer Treaty with Great Britain ratified

BORN: September 21, 1788
BIRTHPLACE: Calvert County, Maryland
PARENTS: Walter and Ann Mackall Smith
MARRIED: Zachary Taylor, 1810
CHILDREN: 1 son, 5 daughters
DIED: August 18, 1852. Age, 63

Margaret Taylor

Maiden Name : Margaret Mackall Smith

MARGARET TAYLOR belongs to the group of First Ladies who lived most of their lives on the frontier. She was born in 1788 in Maryland, the daughter of a major in the Continental Army, but little is known of her childhood. After the death of her father when she was 12 years old, she apparently went to live with a married sister on the Kentucky frontier, and it was here that she met the young soldier, Zachary Taylor. They were married on June 21, 1810.

In the years that followed, Margaret went with her husband from one frontier garrison to another, for Taylor rapidly made a name for himself in the army and was being steadily advanced. They rarely stayed in any one location long enough to make a real home, and as the children were born, Margaret usually sent them back to Kentucky or Virginia, as soon as they were old enough to live with relatives. For twenty years or more Margaret lived the life of a frontier soldier's wife at army posts in Wisconsin, in Louisiana, in Michigan, and in Florida. She shared with her husband the dangers of frontier life and often went about her household tasks with a pistol in her apron pocket. In the wars against Indians, she took an active part in nursing the sick and wounded. In 1841 General Taylor was stationed at Baton Rouge, La., and here Margaret was at last able to make a home. Six children had been born to them, but only three had survived.

Margaret would have been happy to continue living quietly in the home in Baton Rouge, but General Taylor's victories during the war with Mexico made him a national hero, and in 1848 the Whig party persuaded him to be their candidate for President. When he was elected, Margaret accompanied him to the White House, but she left most of the entertaining to her youngest daughter, Betty. Margaret herself usually took part only in the more formal public functions where her presence was expected. She had been strongly opposed to having her husband run for the Presidency, and she now felt that the responsibilities of the office might be too heavy for a man of his age. In this she was proved right, for President Taylor fell ill and died after only 16 months in office.

After his death Margaret returned to Louisiana to live with her only son, Richard. She died two years later in 1852.

*Let us remember that revolutions
do not always establish freedom.*
—ADDRESS TO CONGRESS, 1852

Millard Fillmore

13th President, 1850–1853 — Party: Whig

BORN: January 7, 1800

BIRTHPLACE: Summerhill, New York

PARENTS: Nathaniel and Phoebe Millard Fillmore

EDUCATION: Self-taught

RELIGION: Unitarian

OCCUPATION: Lawyer

MARRIED: Abigail Powers, 1826
Caroline McIntosh, 1858

AGE AT INAUGURATION: 50

TERM OF OFFICE: 2 years, 8 months

DIED: March 8, 1874. Age, 74

MILLARD FILLMORE was another "log cabin" President and came to the White House through the untimely death of President Taylor. Fillmore grew up in a small farming community in New York State and had little opportunity for schooling. He was "bound out" to learn the trade of a wool carder, and when about 19 years old fell in love with the village schoolteacher, Abigail Powers. She encouraged him to educate himself, and his ambition was fostered by a judge in his home town, who helped him to become a lawyer. He was 32 when admitted to the bar, but had already had some experience in state politics, and he now went on to hold a succession of political offices. He served five terms in the U. S. House of Representatives; ran for the office of Governor of New York in 1844 but was defeated; and then served as Comptroller of New York. In 1848, when Zachary Taylor was nominated for President by the Whigs, Fillmore was selected as the candidate for Vice President. Sixteen months after the inauguration Taylor died, and Fillmore became the 13th President.

Fillmore came into office just at the time when the debates in Congress over the extension of slavery to the newly acquired western territories were at their height. Although personally against slavery, Fillmore supported the Compromise of 1850, which provided for the entry of California as a free state in return for a strict "Fugitive Slave" act to force the return of runaway slaves. This compromise complicated the sensitive question even more, and split both the Whig and the Democratic parties. More constructive events of his administration were the opening of trade with Japan and the growth of the West.

Fillmore was not renominated in 1852, and so passed out of office after serving only two years and eight months as President. He was, in fact, the last Whig President, for the Whig party, split by the slavery question, never regained power. He tried for renomination again four years later as the candidate of the "Know-Nothing" party, but carried only one state. After this, Fillmore retired to private life. He died in Buffalo, N. Y., when 74 years old.

PUBLIC CAREER

Member of New York Assembly; member of U.S. House of Representatives; comptroller of New York State; Vice President; President.

ADMINISTRATION EVENTS

1850 California admitted to Union
Fugitive Slave Act passed

1852 Commodore Perry sent to Japan to open trade negotiations

BORN: March 13, 1798
BIRTHPLACE: Stillwater, New York
PARENTS: Lemuel and Abigail Newland Powers
MARRIED: Millard Fillmore, 1826
CHILDREN: 1 son, 1 daughter
DIED: March 30, 1853. Age, 55

Abigail Fillmore

Maiden Name : Abigail Powers

MILLARD FILLMORE married twice, but it was Abigail, his first wife, who was First Lady during his brief term as President.

Their romance was an unusual one, for they met as teacher and pupil in a country school. Abigail was the daughter of a Baptist minister in Saratoga County, N. Y. Her father died when she was quite young, and when Abigail was 16, she became a teacher in the village school. Here, a year or two later, came the farm boy, Millard Fillmore, anxious to gain an education. He was about 17 years old at this time, but had never had any schooling. Abigail encouraged and helped him and it was not long before they fell in love. They were married in 1826, after a courtship of eight years. Since both were poor, Abigail continued to teach school as well as take care of her home, and she also tutored her husband while he studied to become a lawyer.

In 1830 they moved to Buffalo, N. Y. where Abigail's second child, a girl, was born. She now had more leisure, for her husband was making a successful career in politics, and she took up the study of French and music. She also accompanied her husband to sessions of the New York Assembly in Albany, and to meetings of the U. S. Congress in Washington. In 1848 when Fillmore was elected as Vice President under President Zachary Taylor, Margaret went to make her home in Washington. Only a year and a half later, after the death of President Taylor, she became First Lady.

Abigail proved to be a very competent mistress of the White House. She was dignified and commanding in bearing, and had wide intellectual interests. Ill health, however, frequently made it necessary for her daughter to act as hostess.

Abigail also took a number of steps to make the White House more comfortable. She had water pipes installed and purchased new carpeting and furniture. Then, discovering that there were no books in the White House, she set aside a big cheerful room as a library, and carefully chose the books to fill its bookcases. This collection later became the nucleus of the present White House library.

Fillmore left office after filling out Taylor's uncompleted term. At the inauguration ceremony for his successor, Franklin Pierce, Abigail took cold and became fatally ill. She died in Washington on March 30, 1853, and was buried in Buffalo.

Millard Fillmore's second wife was Caroline Carmichael McIntosh, a widow, whom he married in 1858. She survived him by seven years, dying in 1881.

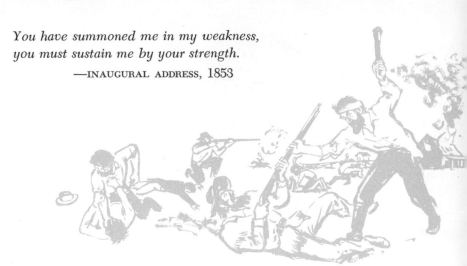

You have summoned me in my weakness,
you must sustain me by your strength.

—INAUGURAL ADDRESS, 1853

Franklin Pierce

14th President, 1853-1857 — Party: Democratic

BORN: November 23, 1804
BIRTHPLACE: Hillsboro, New Hampshire
PARENTS: Benjamin and Anna Kendrick Pierce
EDUCATION: Bowdoin College
RELIGION: Episcopalian

OCCUPATION: Lawyer
MARRIED: Jane M. Appleton, 1834
AGE AT INAUGURATION: 48
TERMS OF OFFICE: One (4 years)
DIED: October 8, 1869. Age, 64

FRANKLIN PIERCE, known as "Young Hickory of the Granite Hills," was our first President to hail from the state of New Hampshire, of which his father (who had fought in the Revolutionary War) was Governor. Giving up his original ambition to be a soldier, he attended Bowdoin College, and became a lawyer instead. Handsome and likeable, with many friends, he won political office easily. After serving as a member of his state legislature, he was twice elected to Congress, and became a Senator at the age of 33. Later he refused a second term and also declined the offer of a place in President Polk's Cabinet.

When the Mexican War broke out, Pierce enlisted as a private, but was made a brigadier general the next year, and led his forces with distinction in the battles of Contreras and Churubusco.

After returning home from the war, Pierce did not seek further public office, but he was nominated by the Democrats as a "dark horse" candidate for President in the Convention of 1852. The Whig party was badly disorganized by this time, and Pierce won a sweeping victory.

Although a Northerner by birth, Pierce's political ties were chiefly with the South. The struggle over the extension of slavery was becoming increasingly bitter, and Pierce supported and signed the Kansas-Nebraska Bill, allowing those territories to decide for themselves whether they would be slave or free. Although he had hoped this would permit a peaceful settlement of the question, it actually only stirred up more trouble between the pro- and anti-slavery factions.

Pierce did, however, succeed in settling the Mexican boundary question by the Gadsen Purchase, which added 45,000 square miles to the United States. He also rejected the Ostend Manifesto to sieze Cuba, negotiated a trade treaty with Japan, and worked for an effective foreign policy.

Pierce was not renominated, and after retiring from the Presidency he traveled extensively in Europe. When the Civil War started, he urged loyalty to the Union, although he himself was a slave owner. He died and was buried in Concord, N. H., in 1869.

PUBLIC CAREER

Member of New Hampshire legislature; member of U. S. House of Representatives; U. S. Senator; Brigadier General, U. S. Army; President.

ADMINISTRATION EVENTS

1854 Trade treaty with Japan ratified
Kansas-Nebraska Bill enacted
Gadsen Purchase negotiated

BORN: March 12, 1806
BIRTHPLACE: Hampton, New Hampshire
PARENTS: Jesse and Elizabeth Appleton
MARRIED: Franklin Pierce, 1834
CHILDREN: 3 sons
DIED: December 2, 1863. Age, 57

Jane Pierce

Maiden Name : Jane Appleton

JANE APPLETON PIERCE, President Pierce's First Lady, was a very different type of person from her gay and lively husband. Shy and sensitive, she preferred a quiet, sheltered life to the social demands of a political career.

Jane Appleton was born in Hampton, N. H. Her father, a Congregational minister and president of Bowdoin College, was an intensely religious man, and her mother was a member of a well-to-do family of Amherst, Mass. After her father's death from tuberculosis when she was 13 years old, Jane's mother returned to Amherst, and Jane grew up there in quiet, cultural surroundings. When she was about 20 years old, she met Franklin Pierce, a graduate of Bowdoin College, who was studying law in Northampton. Jane was a shy, delicately beautiful girl; Franklin a handsome, dashing young man of the world, and they attracted each other as opposites often do. It was six years, however, before they were married, which suggests that Pierce may have had some difficulty in winning the consent of Jane's strict and religious relatives.

At the time of their marriage, in 1834, Pierce was a member of the U. S. House of Representatives, and in 1836 he was elected to the U. S. Senate, but Jane spent little time in Washington. She preferred their home in Concord, N.H., where she devoted herself to the care of their two sons. A third child, also a boy, had died in infancy. Because of her dislike of public life she repeatedly urged her husband to give up politics and return to the practice of law, and at last in 1842 he agreed to do so. In 1846, when the Mexican War broke out, he immediately joined the army and

served with distinction in the campaigns in Mexico, but on his return he took up his law practice again and declined several offers of political office. In 1852, however, he was practically drafted as the "dark horse" Democratic candidate for the Presidency and was elected.

Jane's natural pride and pleasure in this honor was destroyed by a tragic occurrence a few days before the inauguration, when their only surviving son, Benny, was killed in a railway accident. It was weeks before she was able to join her husband in Washington, and she never fully recovered from her grief. Her natural shyness as well as her failing health made it difficult for her to carry out the social duties of a First Lady.

After President Pierce retired from office in 1857, they traveled abroad for about two years, then returned to their New England home. Jane died in Andover, Mass., in 1863, and was buried in Concord.

Next in importance to the maintenance of the Constitution and the Union is the duty of preserving the government free from the taint or even the suspicion of corruption.
—INAUGURAL ADDRESS

James Buchanan

15th President, 1857–1861 — Party: Democratic

BORN: April 23, 1791
BIRTHPLACE: near Mercersburg, Pennsylvania
PARENTS: James and Elizabeth Speer Buchanan
EDUCATION: Dickinson College
RELIGION: Presbyterian

OCCUPATION: Lawyer
MARRIED: (Unmarried)
AGE AT INAUGURATION: 65
TERMS OF OFFICE: One (4 years)
DIED: June 1, 1868. Age, 77

JAMES BUCHANAN was our only bachelor President. He was born near Mercersburg, Pa., where his father was a country storekeeper, attended Dickinson College, and after graduation took up the study of law. He became engaged at this time, but a quarrel separated the two young people, and the girl then died suddenly. This unhappy affair cast a shadow over Buchanan's whole life and he never married.

Buchanan had a long career of public service before coming to the Presidency. During the War of 1812, he fought against the British in the defense of Baltimore. He was elected to the Pennsylvania legislature, and later served in both Houses of Congress. He also served as Minister to Russia and to Great Britain, and was Secretary of State in President Polk's Cabinet.

The presidential nomination for the Democratic party came to Buchanan in 1856. He had been absent from the country for several years as Minister to Great Britain, and hence had not been personally involved in the bitter political battles over the slavery question. As President, Buchanan sought to patch up the quarrels by conference and compromise, but the United States was already a "house divided against itself." Lincoln and Douglas were debating the slavery question in Illinois. The Supreme Court had ruled in its decision on the Dred Scott case that Congress had no power to keep slavery out of the territories. Kansas rejected statehood with slavery. John Brown staged his Harper's Ferry raid to incite a revolt of the slaves, and was hanged for treason. The crisis of civil war was rapidly approaching and President Buchanan could find no way to check it. When he retired from office in March of 1861, the Southern states had already seceded and the Confederacy had been formed. Buchanan lived through the years of the Civil War and died in 1868 at his home near Lancaster, Pa.

PUBLIC CAREER

Member of Pennsylvania legislature; member of U.S. House of Representatives; Minister to Russia; member of U. S. Senate; Secretary of State; Minister to England; President.

ADMINISTRATION EVENTS

1857 Dred Scott decision announced
1858 Lincoln-Douglas debates
Minnesota admitted to Union
1859 John Brown's raid on Harper's Ferry
Oregon admitted to Union
1860 South Carolina seceded from Union
1861 Kansas admitted to Union
Confederate States of America organized

BORN: 1833
BIRTHPLACE: Mercersburg, Pennsylvania
PARENTS: Elliot T. and Jane Buchanan Lane
MARRIED: Henry Elliott Johnston, 1866
CHILDREN: 1 son
DIED: 1903

Harriet Lane

Niece of President James Buchanan

SINCE President Buchanan lived and died a bachelor, there was no official First Lady during his administration. The position of hostess for the President was filled by his niece, Harriet Lane, the daughter of President Buchanan's sister, Jane Buchanan Lane. Her parents died when she was nine years old, though leaving her well-provided with money, and her uncle became her guardian. He saw that she was well educated, and she grew to be a gracious and beautiful young woman, with blonde hair and violet eyes which soon created a sensation in social circles.

Harriet Lane accompanied her uncle to England when he was appointed U. S. Minister there in 1853, and when he was elected to the Presidency she became his official hostess.

Beautiful, charming, and gay of spirit, Harriet was immensely popular and successful in her role of substitute First Lady. She entertained brilliantly and was a leader in Washington society, recalling the days of the celebrated Dolley Madison. Perhaps the crowning event of her years in the White House was the visit of the Prince of Wales.

President Buchanan left office in 1861 after a troubled and unhappy term of office and retired to his home in Pennsylvania. Harriet Lane was married in 1866 to Henry Elliott Johnston, and they had one son, who died in 1881. Harriet herself lived to be seventy years old, dying in 1903.

Although Buchanan was abused and discredited by many for his shortcomings as a President, Harriet Lane remained unwaveringly faithful in her loyalty to the uncle who had brought her up. In her will she bequeathed $100,000 to erect a monument to his memory in Washington.

We here highly resolve that this nation, under God, shall have a new birth of freedom, and that government of the people, by the people, for the people, shall not perish from the earth.

—GETTYSBURG ADDRESS

Abraham Lincoln

16th President, 1861–1865 — Party: Republican

BORN: February 12, 1809
BIRTHPLACE: Near Hodgenville, Kentucky
PARENTS: Thomas and Nancy Hanks Lincoln
EDUCATION: Self-educated
RELIGION: Not a church member

OCCUPATION: Lawyer
MARRIED: Mary Todd, 1842
AGE AT INAUGURATION: 52
TERMS OF OFFICE: One (4 years, 42 days)
DIED: April 15, 1865. Age, 56

TO MOST Americans the name of Abraham Lincoln holds a special place in the list of our Presidents. His greatest achievement politically was in preserving the Union, but it was his humanity and moral greatness that won the love of the people.

Lincoln was a backwoods boy raised in poverty. His parents moved from Kentucky to Indiana when he was seven, and this was his home for 14 years. His mother died when he was quite young, but his understanding stepmother encouraged his ambition to improve himself. Although he had only a few months of schooling, he studied every book he could find or borrow. After the family moved to Illinois in 1830, he worked as a storekeeper and postmaster while studying to become a lawyer. He was elected to one term in the Illinois General Assembly, and in 1837 he moved to Springfield, where he married Mary Todd in 1842. He was elected to Congress for one term (1847-49) as a Whig, but on failing to be re-elected he returned to Illinois.

Lincoln came to national attention as a result of his famous series of debates with Stephen A. Douglas during the senatorial campaign of 1858. He upheld the principle of the supremacy of the Union, and opposed the admission of any more slave states. Douglas won the senatorial election,

but in 1860 Lincoln was nominated for the Presidency by the Republican party.

The Civil War began almost immediately after Lincoln's inauguration in 1861, and for the next five years he was engaged with the problems of this great struggle, both military and political. He acted always in what he thought was the best interests of the country, braving criticism and opposition in the North as well as the South. In 1863 he issued the Emancipation Proclamation, freeing the Negro slaves. The tide of victory began to turn in favor of the North this same year, and in 1864 Lincoln was re-elected for a second term. The war ended with the surrender of Lee on April 9, 1865, but six days later Lincoln was assassinated in Ford's Theatre, Washington. Secretary of War Stanton paid him a fitting tribute when he said, "Now he belongs to the ages."

PUBLIC CAREER

Member of Illinois legislature; member of U. S. Congress; President.

ADMINISTRATION EVENTS

1861 Attack on Fort Sumter
Secession of Southern states
1863 Emancipation Proclamation
1864 Sherman's march to the sea
Nevada admitted to Union
1865 Surrender of Lee

BORN: December 13, 1818
BIRTHPLACE: Lexington, Kentucky
PARENTS: Robert and Eliza Parker Todd
MARRIED: Abraham Lincoln, 1842
CHILDREN: 4 sons
DIED: July 16, 1882. Age, 63

Mary Lincoln

Maiden Name : Mary Todd

MARY TODD, wife of President Lincoln, was born in Lexington, Ky., in 1818. Her father was a well-to-do lawyer and politician, but as her mother died when she was a small child, Mary was brought up by an aunt. She was sent to boarding school and a finishing school, and grew up to be a beautiful but strong-willed girl.

In 1839, when she was 21, Mary went to Springfield, Ill., to live with a sister, and here she met Lincoln, who was just beginning his career as a struggling young lawyer. Mary had announced, perhaps jokingly, that she intended to marry a man who would become President, yet she refused Stephen A. Douglas in favor of the unknown, awkward Lincoln. They were married on Nov. 4, 1842, and began a married life together that was often stormy, marred by Mary's quick temper, jealousy, and social ambitions. Yet in spite of the many unhappy and tragic events in their lives, biographers now believe that there was a bond of true love between Lincoln and Mary.

The Lincolns lived in Springfield until 1861, and it was here that Mary's four sons were born. When at last she reached the White House, she found that her position as First Lady lacked the splendor of which she had so often dreamed. She was the wife of a war-time President, and there were few social functions at the White House. Disappointment over the failure of her social ambitions, and grief over the death of her son Willie affected her disposition in such a way that she antagonized many people.

When Lincoln was elected for a second term, and with the end of the war in sight, Mary un-

doubtedly looked forward to a period when she would at last be able to enjoy her position as First Lady. But the assassination of the President brought a cruel end to these dreams, too, and Mary found herself a widow burdened with heavy debts, for she had always been reckless in her spending.

Mary survived Lincoln by seventeen years, but they were years of sorrow and sickness, both physical and mental. Lincoln had left a comfortable estate, but she was haunted by a fear of poverty. The death of her son Tad was a further blow, and in 1875 her oldest son, Robert, was obliged to place her in a sanitarium. A year later she was released, and for the next few years she lived abroad. In 1880 she returned to live with her sister in Springfield, and two years later she died of a stroke.

The best energies of my life have been spent in endeavoring to establish and perpetuate the blessings of free government.
—INAUGURAL ADDRESS

Andrew Johnson

17th President, 1865–1869 — Party: Democratic

BORN: December 29, 1808
BIRTHPLACE: Raleigh, North Carolina
PARENTS: Jacob and Mary McDonough Johnson
EDUCATION: Self-educated
RELIGION: Methodist? (not a church member)

OCCUPATION: Tailor
MARRIED: Eliza McCardle, 1827
AGE AT INAUGURATION: 56
TERMS OF OFFICE: One (3 years, 323 days)
DIED: July 31, 1875. Age, 66

ANDREW JOHNSON, who succeeded to the Presidency after the assassination of Abraham Lincoln, is remembered chiefly as the only President ever to be impeached.

Johnson was an entirely self-made man. His father died when he was very young and his mother was so poor she was never able to send him to school. He was apprenticed to a tailor, and later, when his mother moved to Greeneville, Tenn., he opened up a shop of his own. In Greeneville he met a schoolteacher, Eliza McCardle, and they were married when he was 18 years old and she 16. Johnson was at this time still illiterate, but like Abraham Lincoln, he was ambitious and eager to learn. Eliza taught him to read and write and encouraged his attempts at debating and oratory. Andrew's shop became a meeting place for people interested in public affairs, and he was soon taking part in local politics. In 1835 he was elected to the Tennessee legislature, and from there he went on to become a U. S. Representative, Governor of Tennessee, and U. S. Senator from Tennessee.

When the Civil War broke out Johnson, although a Southerner, supported the Union. In recognition of his loyalty, Lincoln appointed him military governor of Tennessee in 1862, and two years later he was elected Vice President on the Republican ticket, although he was a Democrat.

As President, Johnson attempted to carry out Lincoln's generous policy toward the defeated South, but Congress insisted on passing its own Reconstruction program over his veto. Congress also passed a Tenure of Office act, which ruled that the President could not remove his own appointees from office without the approval of Congress. When Johnson defied this act by dismissing Secretary of War Stanton, Congress impeached him. In the trial that followed, Johnson was acquitted by only one vote.

Johnson finished out his term as President, but was not re-elected, and in several attempts to win a seat in Congress he was defeated. Finally in 1874 he was again elected to the Senate, but he died on July 31 of the following year.

PUBLIC CAREER

Member of Tennessee legislature; state senator; U. S. Representative; Governor of Tennessee; U. S. Senator; Military Governor of Tennessee; Vice President; President.

ADMINISTRATION EVENTS

1865 Thirteenth Amendment ratified
1867 Nebraska admitted to Union
　　　Reconstruction Acts passed
1868 Impeachment trial of President Johnson
　　　Fourteenth Amendment ratified

BORN: October 4, 1810
BIRTHPLACE: Leesburg, Tennessee
MARRIED: Andrew Johnson, 1827
CHILDREN: 3 sons, 2 daughters
DIED: January 15, 1876. Age, 65

Eliza Johnson

Maiden Name : Eliza McCardle

ELIZA McCARDLE was born in Leesburg, Tenn., in 1810. Her father, a shoemaker, died when she was a small child, and after growing up in the care of a devoted mother, Eliza became a schoolteacher. In Greeneville, Tenn., when she was 16 years old, she met the ambitious young Andrew Johnson, who had opened a tailor shop there. Schoolmistress Eliza soon found out that Andrew had never gone to school and was only then making his first efforts to learn to read and write. She became his teacher as well as his fiancee, and found him an apt and eager pupil. Noticing his special interest in political questions, she aided him by reading accounts of political developments, government matters, and the important speeches of prominent men.

Eliza and Andrew were married May 5, 1827, and at first lived in the rooms behind the tailor shop. But by hard work and study he gradually advanced himself, and in a few years they had a comfortable home. Then Andrew began his political career, and Eliza saw her husband advance from one office to another until he became Vice President and then President.

Eliza was now First Lady, but her health was so poor that she was unable to take an active part in the social life of the White House. During the years of the Civil War, when Johnson was being denounced as a traitor to the South, and Eliza was living alone in Greeneville, she suffered greatly from anxiety and loneliness, and the death of one of her sons at this time further broke her health.

Her duties at the White House were taken over most capably by her oldest daughter, Martha Patterson, wife of the Senator from Tennessee, and by her daughter-in-law, Mary Johnson Stover, widow of her dead son. These two young women amazed Washington society by their good taste in redecorating the White House, which had been neglected all during the war years, and by their own charm and elegance of manner.

The strain and turmoil of Johnson's battles with Congress were a further drain on Eliza's health, but she supported him unwaveringly. She never doubted that he would be acquitted of the impeachment charges.

Eliza would have been happy to have her husband retire to private life permanently after his term of office was over, but she was naturally pleased when he was again elected to the Senate as Senator from Tennessee. However, he served only one term, dying in 1875, and she followed him six months later.

I shall on all subjects have a policy to recommend, but none to enforce against the will of the people.

—FIRST INAUGURAL ADDRESS

Ulysses Simpson Grant

18th President, 1869–1877 — Party: Republican

BORN: April 27, 1822
BIRTHPLACE: Point Pleasant, Ohio
PARENTS: Jesse and Hannah Simpson Grant
EDUCATION: U. S. Military Academy, West Point
RELIGION: Methodist

OCCUPATION: Soldier
MARRIED: Julia Dent, 1848
AGE AT INAUGURATION: 46
TERMS OF OFFICE: Two (8 years)
DIED: July 23, 1885. Age, 63

ALTHOUGH several earlier Presidents had won fame as soldiers, Ulysses S. Grant was the first West Point graduate to be elected to the Presidency.

Grant was born at Point Pleasant, Ohio. His father was a tanner, but Grant hated that occupation, and was glad to win an appointment to West Point, where he distinguished himself as a horseman. After receiving his commission he saw active duty in the Mexican War, and was then stationed at garrisons on the Pacific Coast. After several years of duty there he resigned from the army and rejoined his wife (Julia Dent, whom he married in 1848) in St. Louis.

Grant now tried farming and then business to support his family, but failed in everything. At the time the Civil War broke out he was working in his brothers' store in Galena, Ill. Grant immediately volunteered his services and was appointed a brigadier general of Illinois volunteers. This was the turning point of his career and he went on from victory to victory. His leadership and genius for military tactics in the war were largely responsible for the North's victories and Lee's eventual surrender.

Now a national hero, Grant was persuaded to accept the Republican nomination for President in 1868 although he had had no experience in politics. Grant's two terms were filled with many complicated and difficult problems which he was unable to solve—problems of Reconstruction in the South, of political graft in Washington, of financial panics. He was President during a very corrupt period, and his dependence on the advice of friends and politicians resulted in many unwise appointments.

At the end of his two terms of office he made a trip around the world and then entered into partnership with a New York banking firm. It ended in bankruptcy and he lost practically everything he owned. To pay his debts and provide a legacy for his wife, he devoted the last year of his life to writing his memoirs, which he completed just four days before his death, on July 23, 1885. A beautiful tomb, paid for by public subscription, was erected for him in New York City.

PUBLIC CAREER

Major General; Lieutenant General; General of the Army; President.

ADMINISTRATION EVENTS

1869 First transcontinental railway completed
1870 Fifteenth Amendment adopted
1873 Severe financial panic
1876 Custer's Massacre in Montana
Colorado admitted to Union

BORN: January 26, 1826
BIRTHPLACE: St. Louis, Missouri
PARENTS: Frederick and Ellen Wrenshall Dent
MARRIED: Ulysses S. Grant, 1848
CHILDREN: 3 sons, 1 daughter
DIED: December 14, 1902. Age, 76

Julia Grant

Maiden Name: Julia Boggs Dent

JULIA DENT, who became the wife of President Grant, was born in St. Louis, Mo., in 1826. Her father was Judge Frederick Dent, the son of a Revolutionary War officer.

Julia met young Grant when he came to her home to visit her brother, his classmate at West Point. They were married in 1848, just after the close of the war with Mexico, in spite of the misgivings of Julia's father, who did not think much of the prospects of a poorly paid young army officer. The first two years of their marriage were spent at army posts in Michigan; then Grant was sent to the Pacific Coast and Julia returned to St. Louis, as she was expecting a baby.

Possibly because of his loneliness and his anxiety about providing for his family, Grant drank more than was good for him, and eventually he was obliged to resign his commission. He returned home, and for the next ten years he and Julia struggled together against poverty, failure, and debts. Although she had been brought up as the daughter of a well-to-do planter, with servants to relieve her of all work, Julia now cheerfully did the cooking and sewing and household tasks in their farm home near St. Louis and also cared for their four children.

The farm failed, and after two years of unsuccessful attempts at other jobs, Grant was offered work in his brothers' store in Galena. The family now moved to Galena to start a new life, and it was from here that Grant went back into the army. Julia's steadfast faith in her husband was rewarded when he returned to Galena at the end of the war as a famous general with a salary of $29,000 a year. Four years later he was elected

President, and Julia became First Lady.

Her eight years as mistress of the White House were the happiest of Julia Grant's life, as she herself said. She was an admirable hostess, and enjoyed receiving the throngs of guests and visitors who came to the White House to meet her famous husband. When Grant's two terms of office were over, they went on a world tour that lasted almost three years.

On their return, they bought a home in New York City, but within four years Grant's business firm failed and they were again reduced to poverty. However, the *Memoirs* that Grant succeeded in writing before his death provided nearly $500,000 in royalties for Julia.

Julia Grant stood by her husband in poverty, in illness, in military victory and in civilian defeat, before and after those eight happy years in the White House. She survived him by 17 years, and after her death in 1902, she was buried beside him in the tomb on Riverside Drive.

Rutherford Birchard Hayes

19th President, 1877–1881 — Party: Republican

BORN: October 4, 1822
BIRTHPLACE: Delaware, Ohio
PARENTS: Rutherford and Sophia Birchard Hayes
EDUCATION: Kenyon College; Harvard Law School
RELIGION: Attended Methodist Church

OCCUPATION: Lawyer
MARRIED: Lucy Ware Webb, 1852
AGE AT INAUGURATION: 54
TERMS OF OFFICE: One (4 years)
DIED: January 17, 1893. Age, 70

THE LIFE of Rutherford B. Hayes shows none of the dramatic contrasts, the violent ups and downs of fortune that marked the careers of some of the other Presidents. His enemies called him "Goody-good," but he was generally respected for his scholarly tastes and his honesty and dignity.

Hayes was born in Delaware, Ohio, and as his father died before his birth, he was brought up by an uncle, who helped him to secure a good education. He attended Harvard Law School, and after being admitted to the bar, moved to Cincinnati where he practiced law until 1861.

During the Civil War he served as a major of the Ohio Volunteers, took part in a number of battles, was wounded, and won the rank of brigadier general. In 1864 he was elected to the U. S. House of Representatives. In 1868 he became Governor of Ohio and served three terms.

Hayes was now well-known nationally and was nominated for President in 1876 by the Republican party. His opponent was Samuel J. Tilden, Governor of New York, and the electoral vote was so close that the results were disputed and Hayes won by only one vote.

Hayes became President at a critical time when North and South were still nursing ill feelings stemming from the Civil War. He withdrew

Federal troops from the Southern states, and thus gave the South a chance to put its house in order without interference. He also removed from office men that he considered dishonest or incompetent, and attempted to reorganize the government along lines of strict integrity. He supported "sound money" policies and stood firmly against the inflationary measures proposed by Congress.

A new era of national expansion and prosperity was growing during Hayes' administration. "Big business" was developing and great fortunes were being made in steel, oil, and other industries. Immigrants were pouring into the country; and new advances were being made in science.

Hayes did not believe that a President should serve more than one term, and he declined renomination. In 1881 he retired from public life and devoted the rest of his life to educational enterprises and philanthropy. He died at Fremont, Ohio, in 1893, and was buried there.

PUBLIC CAREER
Army officer; member of U. S. House of Representatives; Governor of Ohio; President

ADMINISTRATION EVENTS
1877 Federal troops withdrawn from Southern states
1878 Bland-Allison Act for coinage of silver passed over presidential veto
1879 Electric light bulb invented by Thomas Edison

BORN: August 28, 1831
BIRTHPLACE: Chillicothe, Ohio
PARENTS: James and Maria Cook Webb
MARRIED: Rutherford B. Hayes, 1852
CHILDREN: 7 sons; 1 daughter
DIED: June 25, 1889. Age, 57

Lucy Hayes

Maiden Name : Lucy Ware Webb

THE girl who became Mrs. Rutherford Hayes was Lucy Ware Webb, born in 1831 in Chillicothe, Ohio. Her father was a doctor, and her mother's father had been one of the first settlers of Chillicothe. Through her mother, Lucy was descended from the Puritans of New England.

Lucy Ware Webb was the first college graduate to become a President's wife. It was during these years of the mid-nineteenth century that women's colleges were just beginning, and Lucy attended the Wesleyan Female College in Cincinnati, graduating in 1852. In December of the same year she married Rutherford Hayes, a rising young lawyer of Cincinnati whom she had met at a summer resort during one of her school vacations.

Their married life together, both in Ohio and later in the White House, was serene and happy. Except during the war years, Lucy Hayes was on the whole free from the anxieties and troubles that had surrounded so many of the earlier First Ladies. Hayes was successful as a lawyer, and his career as Governor of Ohio and later as President brought him honor and national respect.

As a college graduate, Lucy was interested in literature and the arts, and also in many of the reform movements that were then rousing the interest of women. She believed in woman suffrage, worked to improve the condition of the underprivileged, and supported the Women's Christian Temperance Union. Neither she nor President Hayes believed in drinking wines or liquors and did not serve them at the White House, which resulted in some members of Washington society giving her the nickname of "Lemonade Lucy."

She took this with good humor, however, and most of her friends respected her and the President for holding to their convictions.

Lucy Hayes was in fact a popular and successful White House hostess. She enjoyed giving parties, especially for young people, and when Congress stopped the practice of having the annual Easter egg-rolling party for children on the Capitol grounds, she immediately invited them to have the party on the White House grounds instead. She dressed simply but elegantly, and thoroughly enjoyed the various public ceremonies she was called on to attend as First Lady.

At the close of Hayes' term of office, they retired to their home in Ohio, where Lucy continued to lead a happy and active life. She devoted much of her time to matters of social welfare, such as improving the public schools. She died on June 25, 1889, at Fremont, Ohio, four years before her husband.

For mere vengeance I would do nothing.
This nation is too great to look for
revenge. But for the security of
the future I would do everything.

—ADDRESS, 1865

James Abram Garfield

20th President, 1881 (6½ months) — Party: Republican

BORN: November 19, 1831
BIRTHPLACE: Orange, Ohio
PARENTS: Abram and Eliza Ballou Garfield
EDUCATION: Williams College
RELIGION: Disciples of Christ

OCCUPATION: Teacher
MARRIED: Lucretia Rudolph, 1858
AGE AT INAUGURATION: 49
TERM OF OFFICE: 6 months
DIED: September 19, 1881. Age, 49

GARFIELD was another President who had to struggle for an education and for a place in life. His parents were pioneer settlers in Ohio. His father died when he was very young and he had to go to work early to help support his widowed mother. Eager for an education, he found ways to work his way through school and through Williams College in Massachusetts, and then returned to Ohio to teach. He became president of Hiram Institute, or College, where he had formerly been a student, but at the same time continued to study law. He was admitted to the bar in 1860, when he was 29 years old.

Like Hayes, Garfield answered Lincoln's call for volunteers in 1861, and like Hayes, too, he distinguished himself for bravery, eventually winning the rank of major-general. The Republican party in Ohio elected him to the U. S. House of Representatives in 1862, and he served in Congress for 17 years. When the Republican party split into two factions known as the "Stalwarts" and the "Half-breeds," he joined with the Half-breeds. At the Republican convention of 1880 the two main candidates for nomination were General Grant, who was being urged by the Stalwarts to run for a third term, and Sen. James G. Blaine, who was the leader of the Half-breed faction.

The convention became deadlocked, and Garfield was then chosen as a compromise candidate, with Chester A. Arthur, a Stalwart, as his running mate for Vice President.

After the election Garfield tried to unite the two factions of his party, but without much success. There was great competition for political jobs in Washington, and Garfield was constantly criticized by both factions of the party for the appointments he made. On July 2, 1881, only four months after he had taken office, a fanatic of the Stalwart group approached him at a railway station in Washington, suddenly pulled out a pistol, and fired. The President was not killed immediately but died two months later on Sept. 19, 1881 at Elberon, N. J.

Whether Garfield would have made a successful President no one can say. In spite of an impressive personal appearance, he perhaps did not have the forcefulness of character needed for national leadership.

PUBLIC CAREER

Ohio state senator; Major General; U. S. Congressman; President.

ADMINISTRATION EVENTS

1881 American Red Cross established
Tuskegee Institute opened.

BORN: April 19, 1832
BIRTHPLACE: Garretsville, Ohio
PARENTS: Zebulon and ? Mason Rudolph
MARRIED: James Garfield, 1858
CHILDREN: 5 sons, 2 daughters
DIED: March 14, 1918. Age, 85

Lucretia Garfield

Maiden Name : Lucretia Rudolph

LUCRETIA ("Crete") Rudolph was born in 1832 near Garretsville, Ohio, the daughter of a prosperous farmer who was one of the founders of Hiram Institute, or College. Her mother was a daughter of Elijah Mason of Lebanon, Conn., and a descendant of Gen. Nathaniel Greene of Revolutionary War fame. Lucretia was a quiet, rather shy girl who loved books and wished to become a teacher. She attended Hiram Institute at the same time James Garfield was working his way through school there, and the two young people became engaged. He was planning to go east to Williams College, however, so they could not be married until he had completed his studies. In the meantime, Lucretia taught school in Cleveland.

They were finally married on Nov. 11, 1858, and made their first home in a little cottage on the campus of Hiram College, where Garfield was teaching Greek and Latin. Even after he became president of the school they had little money, but were happy with books and college activities.

During the war years, while Garfield was on active duty, Lucretia remained busy with home and family affairs, and managed to save enough money to buy a small house. In 1863, however, Garfield went to Washington as a member of the House of Representatives, and Lucretia divided her time between Washington and their home in Ohio.

When Garfield became the surprise candidate for President in 1880, Lucretia was impressed with the responsibility that went with the honor of the office. She worked devotedly for him dur-

ing the months of the campaign, and after the inauguration in 1881 she was prepared to carry out the duties of First Lady with gracious dignity. But almost before she had become accustomed to her new position, it was ended by the assassin's bullet fired at President Garfield. During the long weeks when he was slowly losing strength, she nursed him bravely.

While Garfield was dying, a public subscription fund was started for the benefit of Mrs. Garfield and her family which eventually reached the sum of $350,000—a generous expression of the nation's grief. Mrs. Garfield survived her husband by many years, and lived to see her four sons become successful in their chosen professions and her one daughter happily married.

She died in Pasadena, Calif., on March 14, 1918, at the age of 85 years.

43

The wisdom of our fathers, foreseeing even the most dire possibilites, made sure that the government should never be imperiled because of the uncertainty of human life. Men may die, but the fabric of our free institutions remains unshaken.

—INAUGURAL ADDRESS

Chester Alan Arthur

21st President, 1881–1885 — Party: Republican

BORN: October 5, 1830
BIRTHPLACE: Fairfield, Vermont
PARENTS: William and Malvina Stone Arthur
EDUCATION: Union College
RELIGION: Episcopalian

OCCUPATION: Lawyer
MARRIED: Ellen L. Herndon, 1859
AGE AT INAUGURATION: 50
TERM OF OFFICE: 3 years, 166 days
DIED: November 18, 1886. Age, 56

WHEN President Garfield was assassinated in 1881, Vice President Arthur became President. Arthur had been considered of no particular importance politically when he was chosen to be Garfield's running mate, but as President he showed unexpected strength and leadership.

Arthur was a New Englander, born in Fairfield, Vt., of Scotch-Irish parentage. His father was a Baptist clergyman of scholarly tastes. Young Arthur entered Union College in Schenectady, N. Y., at the age of 15 and graduated in three years. He then taught school for a while and studied law, but politics soon became his real career. During the Civil War, he held an important administrative post as quartermaster general of New York and carried out his duties very efficiently. After the war was over, his ability and energy brought him to the attention of the leaders of the Republican party, and in 1871 President Grant appointed him Collector of the Port of New York, an important position which controlled the patronage of many small political jobs. When President Hayes tried to put this office under Civil Service, Arthur fought to continue the "spoils system" and was removed from office.

When Arthur was nominated for Vice President, he was a follower of Roscoe Conkling, New York's powerful political boss and leader of the "Stalwart" faction of the Republicans. But after Arthur became President he surprised everyone by putting party politics aside and administering the government fairly and conscientiously. He actively supported the Civil Service Reform Act, insisted on using surplus revenues to reduce the national debt, and urged the reduction of taxes. The politicians who had expected spoils and patronage from him were angered, but the public applauded him as President of the whole people. Arthur's administration was also marked by continued industrial expansion.

Yet, in spite of his creditable performance as President, Arthur could not hold the support of his party, and he was not nominated in 1884 for a term in his own right. He returned to his law practice in New York City, and died one year later at the age of 56 years.

PUBLIC CAREER

Quartermaster General, New York State Militia; Collector of the Port of New York; Vice President; President.

ADMINISTRATION EVENTS

1883 Civil Service Commission organized
1884 Establishment of territorial government in Alaska
1885 Washington Monument dedicated

BORN: August 30, 1837
BIRTHPLACE: Fredericksburg, Virginia
PARENTS: William Lewis and
　Frances Hansbrough Herndon
MARRIED: Chester A. Arthur, 1859
CHILDREN: 2 sons, 1 daughter
DIED: January 12, 1880. Age, 42 years

Ellen Arthur

Maiden Name: Ellen Lewis Herndon

ELLEN ARTHUR did not live to enter the White House as First Lady, but undoubtedly she held that title in her husband's eyes. He never remarried after her death, just a year before he became President, and he kept her room in their New York home untouched, a shrine to her memory. She is described as a warmhearted and generous woman.

Ellen Herndon was a Virginian by birth. Her father was Commander William Lewis Herndon of the U. S. Navy, who won fame for his exploration of the Amazon River in 1857, and who later went down with his ship in a gale. Most of her girlhood was spent in Fredericksburg, Va., but on a visit to some relatives in New York she became acquainted with Chester Arthur and they were married on Oct. 29, 1859. Arthur, then 29 years old, had already established a good law practice and was beginning his political career.

In the years that followed, Ellen Arthur became well-known in New York society as a lady of aristocratic background with a sincere interest in the work of various charitable societies. Three children were born to the Arthurs, two sons and one daughter.

Because of her beautiful contralto voice, Mrs. Arthur was often called upon to sing at concerts given to raise money for charity. On one such occasion, on a cold winter night of January, 1880, she took cold, and died three days later of pneumonia. Her marriage had lasted over 20 years.

Had she lived to become First Lady, the Arthurs would undoubtedly have dazzled Washington society. President Arthur was himself an exceptionally handsome man, with gallant manners and a taste for luxurious living. One of his first acts on becoming President was to order the complete redecoration of the White House, and throughout his administration he entertained on a lavish scale. Ellen could have filled her place in such surroundings graciously and efficiently. And there is evidence that Arthur never forgot her. He kept her picture by his bedside and placed fresh flowers before it each day.

Since there was no First Lady, the position of White House hostess was filled by President Arthur's sister, Mary Arthur McElroy. She was a quiet and gentle woman and soon won the admiration and respect of Washington society.

Every citizen owes to the country a vigilant watch and close scrutiny of its public servants and a fair and reasonable estimate of their fidelity and usefulness.

—INAUGURAL ADDRESS

Grover Cleveland

22nd and 24th President, 1885–1889; 1893–1897 — Party: Democratic

BORN: March 18, 1837
BIRTHPLACE: Caldwell, New Jersey
PARENTS: Richard and Anne Neal Cleveland
RELIGION: Presbyterian
EDUCATION: Public schools

OCCUPATIONS: Teacher, lawyer
MARRIED: Frances Folsom, 1886
AGE AT INAUGURATION: 47
TERMS OF OFFICE: Two (8 years)
DIED: June 24, 1908. Age, 71

GROVER CLEVELAND was our only President to serve two non-consecutive terms. He was also the first Democratic President to be elected since 1856.

Cleveland was the son of a Congregational minister, who died when Grover was 16 years old. Since he had to help support his mother and younger brothers and sisters, he was not able to go to college. An uncle helped him find work in Buffalo, and he also studied law. He entered politics as a member of the Democratic party and was elected assistant district attorney, county sheriff, and mayor of Buffalo. The public admired him for his courage in carrying out needed reforms, and for his honesty in an era of graft and corruption. In 1882 he was elected Governor of New York, and the following year he won the Democratic nomination for the Presidency.

As President, Cleveland lived up to his belief that "a public office is a public trust." He became famous as a "veto president," refusing to sign bills that he considered mere raids on the treasury. He fought graft and special privilege and worked for tariff reduction, or "free trade." His stand against patronage and his tariff views made him unpopular with many elements in his party, and in the election of 1888 he was defeated by the Republican candidate, Benjamin Harrison.

Four years later, however, Cleveland was again the Democratic candidate and was again elected. His second administration was marked by the severe financial panic of 1893; the Pullman strike in Chicago, which he put down by sending in Federal troops to protect the mails; and his stubborn fight to maintain the gold standard against the silver interests.

By the end of his second term, Cleveland realized that the best of intentions are not always appreciated. He left the White House on bad terms with his own party and retired to his home at Princeton, N. J. Here he became a trustee of Princeton University and a friend of its president, Woodrow Wilson. When he died in 1908 his last words were, "I have tried so hard to do right!"

PUBLIC CAREER

Assistant district attorney; sheriff; mayor of Buffalo; Governor of New York; President.

ADMINISTRATION EVENTS

1886 Statue of Liberty dedicated
American Federation of Labor organized
1893 Financial panic
Sherman Silver Purchase Act repealed
1894 Pullman Strike
1896 Utah admitted to Union

BORN: July 21, 1864
BIRTHPLACE: Buffalo, New York
PARENTS: Oscar and Emma Harmon Folsom
MARRIED: Grover Cleveland, 1886
    Thomas J. Preston, Jr., 1913
CHILDREN: 2 sons, 3 daughters
DIED: October 29, 1947. Age, 83

Frances Cleveland

Maiden Name : Frances Folsom

LIKE James Buchanan, President Cleveland was a bachelor when he came to the White House, but he did not remain one long. His bride was Frances Folsom, the daughter of his law partner.

Frances was born in Buffalo, New York, and she had known Grover Cleveland as "Uncle Cleve" most of her life. When she was 11 years old her father was killed suddenly, and Cleveland became the administrator of his estate and Frances' guardian. Since he had no family of his own, he spent much of his time at the Folsom home, and he and Frances grew fond of each other. She was not quite 21 when he was inaugurated as President.

The respect and affection that had grown up over so many years now ripened into love, and Frances and President Cleveland were married on June 2, 1886. The whole nation was interested in the romance, for this was the first time that a President had actually been married in the White House. In spite of the difference in their ages— she was 22 and Cleveland 49 at the time of the marriage—their life together, both in and out of the White House, was a very happy one. Cleveland had been a hero to Frances since her childhood, and he was devoted to her. Frances Cleveland soon developed into a well-poised, dignified, and competent First Lady. She presided graciously over receptions and other White House entertainments, and took an intelligent interest in political affairs.

In the four-year interval between Cleveland's first and second terms, they were able to enjoy the pleasures of private life, but when they returned to the White House in 1893, it seemed quite natural to be there again. Frances had now one child, and a second was born in 1893 at the White House. With two small children to care for, Frances had less time for social activities, but she kept up her interest in political developments, and knew that her husband was having a difficult time. It was probably a relief to her when they were able to retire permanently from public life and begin a new life in Princeton. Other children were born and they had in all three girls and two boys.

When Cleveland died in 1908, Frances was still an attractive woman of 44 years. Five years later she married Thomas J. Preston, Jr., a professor at Princeton University. But until the time of her death in 1947, when she was 83 years old, the public still remembered her as Mrs. Cleveland.

Great lives never go out.
They go on.
—ADDRESS ON GRANT

Benjamin Harrison

23rd President, 1889–1893 — Party: Republican

BORN: August 20, 1833

BIRTHPLACE: North Bend, Ohio

PARENTS: John and Elizabeth Irwin Harrison

EDUCATION: Miami University

RELIGION: Presbyterian

OCCUPATION: Lawyer

MARRIED: Caroline Scott, 1853
Mary Lord, 1896

AGE AT INAUGURATION: 55

TERMS OF OFFICE: One (4 years)

DIED: March 13, 1901. Age, 67

BENJAMIN HARRISON, who was President between Cleveland's first and second terms, was a grandson of William Henry Harrison, our ninth President. He was the only grandson of a President to be elected President.

Harrison was born and grew up in North Bend, Ohio, on a farm near the old family homestead of his famous grandfather. He attended Miami University in Ohio, studied law in Cincinnati, and then moved to Indianapolis, where he became one of the leading lawyers. During the Civil War he marched with Sherman through Georgia and eventually won the rank of brigadier general. At the close of the war he resumed his law practice in Indianapolis, and became active in state and national politics as a staunch Republican. From 1881 to 1887 he served in the U. S. Senate, but was then defeated for re-election and returned to Indianapolis to resume his law practice. In 1888, however, the Republican party chose him as their presidential candidate to oppose Cleveland— partly because it was thought his name would appeal to voters of the mid-west. He won the election, although he received less than half of the popular vote.

Harrison, as a Republican President, reversed many of Cleveland's policies. He approved many pension bills that Cleveland had vetoed; favored high tariffs; and approved the Sherman Silver Purchase Act to please the mining interests of the Western states. The United States was still in a great boom period of expansion. Oklahoma Territory was opened to settlement and six new states were admitted to the Union during Harrison's administration. The Sherman Anti-Trust Act of 1890 was passed to check the growth of "big business," but it was not strong enough to have any effect.

Although an eloquent speaker, Harrison did not have the gift of leadership, and in 1892 he was defeated for re-election by his old opponent, Grover Cleveland. He resumed his practice of law and lived quietly in Indianapolis until his death in 1901. His first wife died while he was still in office; he married again in 1896.

PUBLIC CAREER
Army officer; Brigadier General; U. S. Senator; President.

ADMINISTRATION EVENTS
1889 Territory of Oklahoma opened to settlers
North Dakota, South Dakota, Montana, Washington all admitted to Union
Pan-American Conference held
1890 Sherman Anti-Trust Act passed
Idaho and Wyoming admitted to Union
Sherman Silver Purchase Act passed
McKinley Tariff Act passed

BORN: October 1, 1832
BIRTHPLACE: Oxford, Ohio
PARENTS: John and Mary Potts Scott
MARRIED: Benjamin Harrison, 1853
CHILDREN: 1 son, 1 daughter
DIED: October 25, 1892. Age, 60

Caroline Harrison

Maiden Name : Caroline Scott

PRESIDENT Harrison married twice, but it was his first wife, Caroline, who was First Lady while he was in the White House.

Caroline Scott, like Harrison, was a native of Ohio, and grew up in the town of Oxford, where her father was a Presbyterian minister and head of a school for young ladies. Miami University was also located in Oxford, and Caroline and Benjamin no doubt first met when he was a student there. They were married on Oct. 20, 1853, when he was 20 years old and Caroline 21. They moved at once to Indianapolis, and for the next few years struggled along while Harrison tried to make a start as a lawyer. The Civil War interrupted his career for a time and left him poor and in debt, but it was not long before he re-established himself. After he was elected to the U. S. Senate in 1880 they moved to Washington, and Caroline soon became active and popular in Washington society. She was tall and dignified with a serene face, and she was actively interested in both charity and politics.

When Benjamin Harrison became President, Caroline showed new characteristics as First Lady. Always a good housekeeper, and with years of experience in managing on a small income, she now took complete charge of the White House and insisted on checking waste and extravagance. She also wanted to enlarge the White House but Congress would not agree to this, although it did appropriate enough money to allow her to make necessary repairs and renovations, which she carried out carefully. In addition to these domestic duties, she also gave much time to entertaining and making friends for her husband,

who was unfortunately lacking in social charm. Caroline was dismayed by his decision to run for re-election, but she fell ill of a lung ailment in 1892 and died before his first term of office was over.

Mrs. Benjamin Harrison was the first head of the Daughters of the American Revolution. She is also remembered as the First Lady who had the first Christmas tree in the White House, with gifts for every member of the family and the White House staff. The Harrisons had two children, a son and a daughter.

Benjamin Harrison's second wife was Mary Lord Dimmick, whom he married in 1896. She was the niece of the first Mrs. Harrison, and had lived two years at the White House with her aunt. The second Mrs. Harrison survived her husband by many years, dying in New York in 1948. They had one child, a daughter.

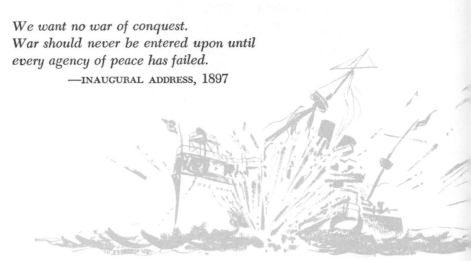

*We want no war of conquest.
War should never be entered upon until
every agency of peace has failed.*
—INAUGURAL ADDRESS, 1897

William McKinley

25th President, 1897–1901 — Party: Republican

BORN: January 29, 1843
BIRTHPLACE: Niles, Ohio
PARENTS: William and Nancy Allison McKinley
EDUCATION: Allegheny College
RELIGION: Methodist

OCCUPATION: Lawyer
MARRIED: Ida Saxton, 1871
AGE AT INAUGURATION: 54
TERMS OF OFFICE: One (4 years, 6 months)
DIED: September 14, 1901. Age, 58

WILLIAM McKINLEY was our third President to die at the hands of an assassin. One of the kindliest of Presidents, he was shot by an anarchist.

William McKinley, like Presidents Hayes and Harrison, was a native of Ohio. He was born at Niles, the son of an iron manufacturer, and received a good education in preparation for becoming a lawyer. At the outbreak of the Civil War he enlisted as a private, served throughout the entire war, and retired with the rank of captain. He then completed his law studies and began practicing in Ohio. In 1876 he was elected to the U. S. House of Representatives, where he served with one brief interruption until 1891. From 1892 to 1896 he was Governor of Ohio, and in 1896 he was nominated on the Republican ticket for the Presidency.

McKinley was always a strong Republican, believing in high tariffs for the protection of American industry. His slogan was "For better times and a full dinner pail." The chief campaign issue, however, was the question whether the United States should hold to the gold standard or adopt a policy of free coinage of silver, as proposed by the Democratic candidate, William Jennings Bryan. The country supported McKinley and the gold standard.

McKinley's first term was a period of progress and prosperity. It was also a time of important foreign events and expansion. In 1898 the sinking of the battleship *Maine* in Havana harbor led to war with Spain. As the result of that war, Cuba became independent and the islands of Puerto Rico, Guam, and the Philippines were ceded to the United States.

In 1900 also McKinley was re-elected for a second term, again defeating Bryan, and seemed about to begin another successful term in which he hoped to promote further expansion of U. S. trade. However, on Sept. 6, 1901, while he was holding a reception at the Pan-American Exposition in Buffalo, a young man approached and shot him without warning. He died a week later. As his body was taken from Washington to Canton, Ohio, for burial, the whole nation mourned.

PUBLIC CAREER

Army officer; county attorney; member of U. S. House of Representatives; Governor of Ohio; President.

ADMINISTRATION EVENTS

1898 U.S.S. *Maine* blown up in Havana harbor
War with Spain
Gold rush in Alaska
1899 Puerto Rico, Guam, Philippines, and Samoa acquired by U. S.

BORN: June 8, 1847
BIRTHPLACE: Canton, Ohio
PARENTS: James and Catherine Dewalt Saxton
MARRIED: William McKinley, 1871
CHILDREN: 2 daughters
DIED: May 26, 1907. Age, 59

Ida McKinley

Maiden Name : Ida Saxton

IDA SAXTON and William McKinley fell in love practically at first sight, and their regard for each other lasted throughout their lives.

Ida Saxton was born in Canton, Ohio, in 1847. Her father was a leading banker in the town, and Ida received a good education, followed by a tour of Europe. On her return, her father, who believed that young women as well as men should be prepared to earn their living, started her to work in his bank as a clerk. She soon became a cashier, and was for three years an assistant to her father.

About this time William McKinley, having completed his law studies, came to Canton to begin his career. He met Ida, then a pretty and light-hearted girl, and fell in love almost immediately. Ida had many other suitors, but she was won by McKinley's ardent courtship, and they were married on Jan. 25, 1871.

Tragedy, however, came to them almost at once. During the first five years of their married life two children were born and died, and Ida's mother also died during these years. These crushing losses broke Ida McKinley's health, and left her with a nervous ailment that caused her to have frequent fainting spells. Her devotion to her husband remained, however, and as he became active in politics she traveled about Ohio with him and kept in touch with everything that was of importance to him. McKinley, on his side, never failed in consideration for her.

After McKinley became President, he kept life at the White House as simple as possible in order to avoid any further strain on his wife's health. She attended official dinners and receptions, where he watched over her carefully, but most other White House entertaining was carried on by other members of the family. Since she was confined to a chair much of the time, she devoted herself to knitting and crocheting fancy goods for charity. In spite of her illness, she maintained a cheerful frame of mind and was always thoughtful of others.

Surrounded by constant and affectionate care, Ida McKinley's years at the White House were happy, and her health even improved a little. In September of 1901, when McKinley was invited to visit the Pan-American Exposition at Buffalo, Ida accompanied him. She was at the home of friends there when word came that the President had been shot down.

Mrs. McKinley survived her husband by less than six years. She was almost continuously ill during this period, and finally died on May 26, 1907. She was buried in Canton beside her husband and their two children.

There can be no fifty-fifty Americanism in this country. There is room here for only 100 per cent Americanism, only for those who are Americans and nothing else.

—ADDRESS AT REPUBLICAN CONVENTION

Theodore Roosevelt

26th President, 1901–1909 — Party: Republican

BORN: October 27, 1858

BIRTHPLACE: New York, New York

PARENTS: Theodore and Martha Bulloch Roosevelt

RELIGION: Dutch Reformed

EDUCATION: Harvard University

OCCUPATIONS: Lawyer, rancher

MARRIED: Alice H. Lee, 1880
Edith Carow, 1886

AGE AT INAUGURATION: 42

TERMS OF OFFICE: Two (7 years, 171 days)

DIED: January 6, 1919. Age, 60

THEODORE ROOSEVELT, who succeeded McKinley, came of an old New York family. As a child he was frail and sickly, but by hard work he built himself up to rugged manhood. After graduating from Harvard and studying law at Columbia, he served two years in the N. Y. State Assembly, then spent two years as a ranchman in North Dakota, living the hard and active outdoor life that he always loved. On his return to New York he threw himself into politics. As a member of the U. S. Civil Service Commission and later as President of the N. Y. Board of Police Commissioners, he fought vigorously against graft and corruption. Appointed Assistant Secretary of the Navy by President McKinley, he reorganized the Navy Department. Then, when war broke out with Spain, he resigned to lead the famous "Rough Riders." He returned home a national hero and was elected Governor of New York, where his vigorous reforms caused alarm to the professional politicians. He was nominated for the Vice Presidency in 1900. Less than a year later McKinley was assassinated and Roosevelt, only 42 years old, became President.

In accordance with his motto to "speak softly and carry a big stick," President Roosevelt fought the trusts, brought railroads under government control, had the Pure Food Act passed, and sup-

ported every measure to conserve national resources. He also got the Panama Canal under way, settled the Alaskan boundary dispute, and negotiated a peace treaty between Russia and Japan for which he received the Nobel Prize. In 1904 he was overwhelmingly elected for a second term, but in 1908 he refused to accept another nomination, giving his support to Taft. He then turned his energies to hunting, travel, and writing. In 1912 he broke with Taft and formed the Progressive or "Bull Moose" party, but was defeated for election.

Even in retirement, Roosevelt maintained his strenuous life. He was an enthusiastic naturalist, a tireless traveler, an explorer and a writer. When he died, Jan. 6, 1919, the nation mourned one of its best-loved Presidents.

PUBLIC CAREER

Member of N.Y. legislature; U.S. Civil Service Commissioner; president, N.Y. Police Commission; Assistant Secretary of Navy; Colonel, U.S. Army; Governor of New York; Vice President; President.

ADMINISTRATION EVENTS

1903 Department of Commerce and Labor established
1904 Panama Canal Zone acquired by U.S.
1905 Russo-Japanese Peace Treaty signed
1906 Federal Pure Food and Drugs Act passed
1907 Oklahoma admitted to Union

BORN: August 6, 1861
BIRTHPLACE: Norwich, Connecticut
PARENTS: Charles and Gertrude Tyler Carow
MARRIED: Theodore Roosevelt, 1886
CHILDREN: 4 sons, 1 daughter
DIED: September 30, 1948. Age, 87

Edith Roosevelt

Maiden Name: Edith Kermit Carow

EDITH ROOSEVELT, who was Theodore Roosevelt's First Lady, was his second wife. His first wife had been Alice Lee, the daughter of George Cabot Lee of Boston, whom he married in 1880, but she had died in 1884. Their one child, Alice, who was a debutante when her father became President, was often called "the Princess of the White House."

Edith Carow was born in Norwich, Conn., in 1861. Her parents were both wealthy and socially prominent, and she had a carefree girlhood and a good education. The Carows and the Roosevelts were well acquainted, and Edith and Theodore knew each other from childhood. After the death of his first wife, Alice Lee, Roosevelt spent two years on his North Dakota ranch, and during that time began to correspond with Edith. Later he journeyed to London to meet her, and they were married there on Dec. 2, 1886. After their honeymoon, spent in travel, they returned to the United States to make their home at Sagamore Hill, overlooking Oyster Bay on Long Island. Five children—four boys and a girl—were born to them in the following years.

When Roosevelt suddenly became President in 1901 the whole family moved into the White House, and the pranks and activities of the Roosevelt children kept all Washington amused. Edith proved to be a charming White House hostess, and also a capable manager of domestic affairs. However, she did not let social duties interfere with her concerns as a wife and mother. She used her influence with her husband to keep him from over-exerting himself, and they both made a point of keeping several hours each day free to spend together with their children.

The whole country took a personal interest in the popular Roosevelt family. When "Princess Alice," the daughter of Alice Lee Roosevelt, was married in the White House to Nicholas Longworth in 1906, it was an occasion for national celebration.

After Roosevelt left office in 1909, he went to Africa on a big-game hunting expedition, while Edith and the children returned to Sagamore Hill. This remained their home for the following years, and Roosevelt died there in 1919.

Now that Edith Roosevelt was a widow and her children grown, she spent much of her time in travel. At last, she finally settled down again at Sagamore Hill, where she shared in the lives of her children and grandchildren and occupied herself with writing her "Odyssey of a Grandmother." She died in 1948, at the age of 87.

*The battlefield as a place of settlement
of disputes is gradually yielding
to arbitral courts of justice.*

—DAWN OF WORLD PEACE

William Howard Taft

27th President, 1909-1913 — Party: Republican

BORN: September 15, 1857
BIRTHPLACE: Cincinnati, Ohio
PARENTS: Alphonse and Louise M. Torrey Taft
EDUCATION: Yale University
RELIGION: Unitarian

OCCUPATION: Lawyer
MARRIED: Helen Herron, 1886
AGE AT INAUGURATION: 51
TERMS OF OFFICE: One (4 years)
DIED: March 8, 1930. Age, 72

WILLIAM HOWARD TAFT was the only President to serve both as President of the United States and as Chief Justice of the Supreme Court.

As the son of a successful lawyer who had been Attorney General under President Grant, Taft turned naturally to the law as a career. After graduating from Yale, he studied law in his father's office, then rose quickly from one office to another. He was a judge in the Superior Court of Cincinnati from 1887 to 1890, then U. S. Solicitor General, then a U. S. Federal Circuit Court judge. In 1900 President McKinley appointed him president of the Philippines Commission following the Spanish American War, and in 1901 he became Governor General of the islands. His success there was so impressive that President Roosevelt appointed him his Secretary of War in 1904, and enthusiastically recommended him to the Republican party as his own successor.

Taft was an able administrator, but he was not a politician and he soon found himself in difficulties with the liberal wing of the Republican party. Although he fought the monopolies, recommended a Federal income tax, and urged lower tariffs, the "progressives" thought him too conservative. In 1912, the dissatisfied Republicans urged Roosevelt to run against Taft for the nomi-

nation. Taft succeeded in winning the nomination with the support of a large body of conservative Republican voters, and Roosevelt then formed the Progressive or "Bull Moose" party, with himself as candidate. This split in the Republican party resulted in the loss of the election, and Woodrow Wilson became President.

After retiring from office, Taft became professor of law at Yale University, president of the American Bar Association, and was finally appointed Chief Justice of the U. S. Supreme Court by President Harding—the office he had always wished to hold. For nine years he enjoyed this honor, and then resigned because of ill health. He died on March 8, 1930.

PUBLIC CAREER

Judge, Superior Court of Cincinnati; U. S. Solicitor General; judge, Federal Circuit Court; President of Philippines Commission; Governor-General of Philippine Islands; Secretary of War; Provisional Governor of Cuba; President; Chief Justice, U.S. Supreme Court.

ADMINISTRATION EVENTS

1909 Robert E. Peary reaches North Pole
1910 Boy Scouts of America incorporated
1912 New Mexico admitted to Union
Arizona admitted to Union
1913 Sixteenth Amendment ratified

BORN: January 2, 1861
BIRTHPLACE: Cincinnati, Ohio
PARENTS: John and Harriet Collins Herron
MARRIED: William Howard Taft, 1886
CHILDREN: 2 sons, 1 daughter
DIED: May 22, 1943. Age, 82

Helen Taft

Maiden Name : Helen Herron

IT WAS Helen Taft, President Taft's First Lady, who planned for the planting of the famous cherry trees around the Tidal Basin in Washington, which are now such a beautiful sight in the spring.

Helen Herron grew up in Cincinnati, where she was born in 1861. Her father was a law partner of Rutherford B. Hayes, who later became President. Helen studied in private schools and became an accomplished pianist. In later years she founded the Cincinnati Symphony Orchestra.

Helen became acquainted with "Will" Taft when she was 18 years old, and after several years of courtship they were married in 1886. In a few years the Tafts were well established in Cincinnati with a family of three children.

In 1900, when Taft was appointed to head the Philippines Commission, Helen and the children accompanied him, and she had her first experience as a "first lady" when her husband became Governor General of the Philippines. Her tact and diplomacy in entertaining the native leaders and their wives were of great help to Taft in winning their trust and friendship.

When Helen Taft became First Lady in 1909, she was quite ready to assume her new duties. She enjoyed social affairs and entertainments, and because of her interest in music often invited leading musicians and singers to the White House as guests. One of the outstanding social occasions of these years was the celebration of the Tafts' silver wedding anniversary at the White House, with some 4,000 guests attending an evening garden party. Remembering the beautiful flowers of the Philippines, she planned to make a similar garden in Potomac Park, and through her efforts the Mayor of Tokyo sent as a gift 3,000 Japanese cherry trees.

Although Helen Taft was naturally ambitious for her husband's success as President, she realized the difficulties of his position, and was prepared for his defeat for re-election. Also, her own health had failed somewhat and her sister often had to act as White House hostess. Their later years, especially after Taft was appointed Chief Justice, were happy and serene. Helen survived her husband for many years, dying in 1943 at the age of 82 years.

*Our whole duty, for the present,
at any rate, is summed up in the motto:
America First.*

—ADDRESS, APRIL 20, 1915

Woodrow Wilson

28th President, 1913–1921 — Party: Democratic

BORN: December 28, 1856

BIRTHPLACE: Staunton, Virginia

PARENTS: Joseph R. and Jessie Woodrow Wilson

EDUCATION: Princeton University

RELIGION: Presbyterian

OCCUPATION: Teacher

MARRIED: Ellen Louise Axson, 1885
Edith Bolling Galt, 1915

AGE AT INAUGURATION: 56

TERMS OF OFFICE: Two (8 years)

DIED· February 3, 1924. Age, 67

WOODROW WILSON, our President during the momentous years of World War I, was a professor of history and political science for 25 years before he entered political life. The son of a Presbyterian minister of Scotch-Irish descent, he was born in Virginia. After graduating from Princeton he studied law, then began his teaching career at Bryn Mawr College in 1885. In 1902 he was elected president of Princeton University, and held this position until 1910, when the New Jersey Democratic party persuaded him to become their candidate for Governor. To the surprise of the machine politicians, he showed himself to be a very able Governor, putting through many needed reforms which brought him to national attention. Two years later he was nominated for the Presidency by the Democrats, and won the election.

As President, Wilson succeeded in getting Congress to pass a number of important acts, such as the Income Tax law, the Federal Reserve System Act, laws regulating trusts and monopolies, the Federal Trade Commission, the Child Labor Law, and other reform measures. When war broke out in Europe in 1914 he at first tried to keep the United States neutral, and the slogan "He kept us out of war" helped to win his reelection in 1916. However, the submarine attacks

of the Germans finally forced the United States to declare war on April 6, 1917.

It was President Wilson who outlined in his famous "Fourteen Points" the terms of surrender which Germany and the Central Powers finally accepted in 1918. He also drew up the plan for a League of Nations and went to Europe in person to present this plan at the peace conference. But though Wilson was successful in establishing the League, the U. S. Senate refused to ratify it, and the United States did not become a member. Bitterly disappointed, Wilson toured the country to win support, but his health broke down and he suffered a stroke. For his last year in office he was an invalid, and he died three years after leaving the Presidency. His efforts were, however, recognized by the award of the Nobel Prize in 1920.

PUBLIC CAREER

Governor of New Jersey; President.

ADMINISTRATION EVENTS

1913 Seventeenth Amendment ratified

1915 *Lusitania* sunk by German submarine

1917 U.S. declares war against Germany

1918 Armistice signed, Nov. 11

1919 Treaty of Versailles
Eighteenth Amendment ratified

1920 Nineteenth Amendment ratified

Ellen Wilson

Maiden Name : Ellen Louise Axson

BORN: May 15, 1860
BIRTHPLACE: Savannah, Georgia
PARENTS: Samuel and Margaret Hoyt Axson
MARRIED: Woodrow Wilson, 1885
CHILDREN: 3 daughters
DIED: August 6, 1914. Age, 54

WOODROW Wilson married twice, and both of his First Ladies played important roles in his life. Ellen Louise Axson, his first wife, was, like himself, the child of a Presbyterian minister, and she had also been born and brought up in the South. They met shortly after Wilson had graduated from Princeton, and the serious-minded student was at once attracted to the quiet, rather shy girl. Two years later, in 1885, they were married and then went to Bryn Mawr, Pa., where Wilson was to teach. During the fol-lowing years, Ellen devoted herself to making a happy and attractive home for her husband. She had artistic tastes, sewed beautifully, and was a charming hostess. Her gracious personality con-tributed much to her husband's popularity and success as president of Princeton University.

Three daughters were born to them, and two were married at the White House after Wilson became President in March, 1913. In 1914, how-ever, Ellen became seriously ill, and died a few days after the outbreak of World War I.

Edith Wilson

Maiden Name : Edith Bolling

BORN: October 15, 1872
BIRTHPLACE: Wytheville, Virginia
PARENTS: William and Sallie White Bolling
MARRIED: Norman Galt, 1896
  Woodrow Wilson, 1915
CHILDREN: none
DIED: December 28, 1961. Age, 89

EDITH BOLLING, who was to become Wil-son's second wife, was born in 1872. She was the daughter of a Virginia judge, and was a direct descendant of Pocahontas and John Rolfe. In 1896 Edith married Norman Galt, a Washington jeweler, but her husband died in 1908. At the time she became acquainted with Woodrow Wil-son she was a strikingly beautiful woman of middle age. Wilson, lonely and unhappy after the death of his first wife, proposed to Edith, and they were married on Dec. 18, 1915.

As First Lady during the most troubled years of Wilson's administration, Edith was the Presi-dent's constant and influential companion. She accompanied him to the peace conference in Eu-rope, supported him when he returned discour-aged, and nursed him devotedly when he fell ill.

After Wilson's term of office was over, they moved to Washington, where he died three years later. Edith Wilson died in 1961 on Dec. 28, her husband's birthday. She was 89, the same age as Anna Harrison (see p. 21).

America's present need is not heroics but healing; not nostrums but normalcy; not revolution but restoration; not surgery but serenity.

—ADDRESS, BOSTON, 1920

Warren Gamaliel Harding

29th President, 1921–1923 — Party: Republican

BORN: November 2, 1865
BIRTHPLACE: Corsica, Ohio
PARENTS: George T. and Phoebe Dickerson Harding
EDUCATION: Ohio Central College
RELIGION: Baptist

OCCUPATION: Newspaper editor
MARRIED: Florence Kling DeWolfe, 1891
AGE AT INAUGURATION: 55
TERM OF OFFICE: Two years, 5 months
DIED: August 2, 1923. Age, 57

WARREN G. HARDING, who was elected on the Republican ticket to succeed Wilson in 1920, was the seventh of our Presidents to be born in Ohio. The son of a rural doctor, he grew up in the town of Marion and attended Ohio Central College, which was actually the equivalent of a high school today. Tall, strongly built, pleasure-loving, and friendly by nature, his chief ambition at this time was to own a newspaper. In 1884, when he was 19 years old, he joined with two friends to buy the bankrupt Marion *Star* for the sum of $300, and thus became an editor. He worked hard at making the newspaper a success, and as he was a good mixer and easily made friends, he was soon taking part in local politics. A loyal supporter of the Republican party, he was elected to the Ohio Senate in 1900, and was elected Lieutenant Governor in 1904. He was defeated when he ran for the office of Governor, but in 1914 he was elected to the U. S. Senate, where he served until 1920.

As a member of the Senate, Harding's genial nature won him many friends, and he was also known as a loyal party man. In 1920, when the Republican convention became deadlocked over the choice of a candidate for the Presidency, Harding was finally proposed as a "dark horse" and was accepted. In the general public reaction at that time against Wilson and the Democratic party, Harding won the election easily.

At first Harding had the confidence of the people, and his slogan, "back to normalcy," was very popular. His most noteworthy accomplishment, however, was the Limitation of Armaments Conference at Washington, to which he invited representatives of the leading nations. Harding also favored having the United States take a part in organizing a World Court. Unfortunately, Harding made some unwise appointments to important offices, and when these men betrayed his trust he was drawn into unsavory political scandals. In 1923 he made a cross-country trip to try to win back public favor, but fell ill in Seattle and died of pneumonia in San Francisco, on Aug. 2. The nation mourned him as a well-meaning man, whatever his shortcomings as a President.

PUBLIC CAREER

Ohio state senator; Lieutenant Governor of Ohio; U. S. Senator; President.

ADMINISTRATION EVENTS

1921 U. S. Budget Bureau created
Dedication of Tomb of Unknown Soldier
1921-22 Conference on Limitation of Armaments at Washington
1923 "Teapot Dome" scandals

BORN: August 15, 1860
BIRTHPLACE: Marion, Ohio
PARENTS: Amos and Louisa Bouton Kling
MARRIED: Henry DeWolfe
   Warren G. Harding, 1891
CHILDREN: 1 son (De Wolfe)
DIED: November 21, 1924. Age, 64

Florence Harding

Maiden Name : Florence Kling

FLORENCE KLING was born in Marion, Ohio, on Aug. 15, 1860. Her father, a successful banker, brought her up as he would have a son, and she was his close companion during her girlhood. She was well educated and taught music for a time until she met and married Henry De Wolfe. This marriage ended in divorce, and she returned home with her one child, a boy, to keep house for her father.

Warren Harding, five years younger than Florence, was at that time just getting started as the editor of the Marion *Star*, and had a reputation for being a rather gay young man-about-town. They met and became engaged, in spite of the strong objections of Florence's father, and were married on July 8, 1891.

Florence Harding was a young woman of ability and ambition, and she did much by her shrewd advice to direct her husband's career. Early in their marriage she offered to help with the work on the newspaper, and for 14 years devoted her energies to making it a success. Undoubtedly she also helped to encourage her husband's political ambitions, and since they had no children she could give his career her full attention. She was devoted to his interests, and although she may have looked forward to the possibility of becoming First Lady, her concern was chiefly for his success.

When Harding was inaugurated, the White House grounds were thrown open to the public in a friendly gesture that increased the President's popularity. Florence Harding gave herself energetically to the duties of entertaining, and she made a point of accompanying her husband to all important public functions.

When criticism of his administration began to become serious, she gave him her loyal sympathy and support. Knowing that he was worried by political attacks, she accompanied him on his last trip across the country, and was beside him when he died.

A little more than a year after the death of her husband, Florence Harding also died. She was buried beside him at the foot of the monument in Marion, Ohio, erected in his honor.

*No nation ever had an army large enough
to guarantee it against attack
in time of peace,
or insure it victory in time of war.*
—ADDRESS, 1925

Calvin Coolidge

30th President, 1923–1929 — Party: Republican

BORN: July 4, 1872
BIRTHPLACE: Plymouth, Vermont
PARENTS: John Calvin and Victoria Moor Coolidge
EDUCATION: Amherst College
RELIGION: Congregationalist

OCCUPATIONS: Lawyer, politician
MARRIED: Grace Anna Goodhue, 1905
AGE AT INAUGURATION: 51
TERM OF OFFICE: One (5 years, 7 months)
DIED: January 5, 1933. Age, 60

CALVIN COOLIDGE was the only President ever to be sworn in by his father. When President Harding died in August, 1923, Vice President Coolidge was vacationing at his boyhood home in Plymouth, Vt., and it was his father, a notary public, who gave him the oath of office.

Calvin Coolidge had grown up as a hard-working farmboy in Vermont. His parents, thrifty New Englanders, sent him to Amherst College, and he then studied law, but soon entered local politics and was steadily elected to one office after another. Although quiet and unemotional, his sturdy honesty and New England common sense appealed to the voters. He was elected to both the Massachusetts House of Representatives and Senate, became Lieutenant Governor in 1916, and Governor in 1919. His resolute stand against the strike by the Boston police force in 1919 won him national acclaim, and in 1920 the Republicans chose him to be Harding's running mate. A year and a half later he succeeded Harding as President.

Americans were impressed with the simplicity and homely virtues of President Coolidge and by his determination to clear up the graft and scandals that he had inherited from the Harding administration. After filling out Harding's term

of office, he was overwhelmingly elected in 1924 for a term in his own right. "Keep Cool with Coolidge" was the campaign slogan.

Coolidge showed his New England thriftiness by setting up government economies which made it possible to reduce the public debt and lower the income tax. The country enjoyed unusual prosperity during his administration, with increasing incomes and a booming stock market. Coolidge could undoubtedly have been elected for a second term, but in 1927 he announced that "I do not choose to run for President in 1928." He held firmly to this decision, declined all attempts to draft him at the convention, and retired quietly from office at the end of his term. The last few years of his life were spent in his native Vermont, where he died on Jan. 5, 1933.

PUBLIC CAREER

Massachusetts state representative; mayor of Northampton; state senator; Lieutenant Governor of Massachusetts; Governor; Vice President; President.

ADMINISTRATION EVENTS

1923-24	"Teapot Dome" scandals
1924	Soldier bonus bill passed over veto
1927	Trans-Atlantic flight by Charles Lindbergh
1929	Kellogg-Briand Peace Pact ratified by U. S.

BORN: January 3, 1879
BIRTHPLACE: Burlington, Vermont
PARENTS: Andrew and Lemira Barnett Goodhue
MARRIED: Calvin Coolidge, 1905
CHILDREN: 2 sons
DIED: July 8, 1957. Age, 78

Grace Coolidge

Maiden Name: Grace Anna Goodhue

GRACE COOLIDGE, President Coolidge's vivacious and sympathetic First Lady, seemed a very different type of person from her husband, yet she too was a native of Vermont and shared many of the same qualities of character. She was born in Burlington, in 1879, and was accustomed to simple ways from her girlhood. After graduating from the University of Vermont in 1902, she became interested in the problems of deaf children and taught for three years at the Clarke School for the Deaf, which was located in Northampton. It was here that she met Calvin Coolidge, and although so different in personalities, the two young people were attracted to each other and were married on Oct. 4, 1905.

Their first home was half of a double house, where they lived very simply and economically for several years. Even after Calvin Coolidge became Governor of Massachusetts, Grace Coolidge and their two sons remained in Northampton, since no home was provided in Boston for the Governor's family. Summer vacations were usually spent at the home of Coolidge's father in Plymouth, Vt. It was at this farm, on Aug. 3, 1923, that Coolidge received the news of Harding's death, and it was here, at 3 o'clock in the morning, that he was sworn in as President.

Grace Coolidge had, of course, had some experience with Washington society before she became First Lady, since she had lived there during the period when her husband was Vice President. She showed very quickly that she was quite capable of handling her new responsibilities as mistress of the White House, although retaining her natural simplicity. Her friendly,

sympathetic nature, warmly democratic manners, and cheerful disposition won friends everywhere, and offset the rather chilly impression given by "Silent Cal." She was a good housekeeper, a gracious hostess, and enjoyed meeting the many visitors who flocked to the White House.

The Coolidges encountered one sad tragedy in the White House. Their younger son, Calvin Coolidge, Jr., developed blood poisoning from a blister on his heel, and died in the summer of 1924. Coolidge's decision not to run for a second term, announced shortly afterwards, was probably due to his concern for his wife's health.

After retiring from the White House, the Coolidges returned to Northampton where they bought an estate which they called "The Beeches." But after her husband's death, Mrs. Coolidge sold The Beeches and built a new home not far from the house where she had first started housekeeping. She died here in July, 1957, at the age of 78.

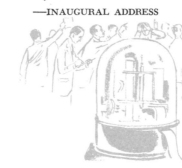

Ours is a land filled with millions of happy homes, blessed with comfort and opportunity. I have no fear for the future of our country. It is bright with hope.

—INAUGURAL ADDRESS

Herbert Clark Hoover

31st President, 1929–1933 — Party: Republican

BORN: August 10, 1874
BIRTHPLACE: West Branch, Iowa
PARENTS: Jesse Clark and Huldah Minthorn Hoover
EDUCATION: Stanford University
RELIGION: Quaker

OCCUPATION: Engineer
MARRIED: Lou Henry, 1899
AGE AT INAUGURATION: 54
TERMS OF OFFICE: One (4 years)
DIED: October 20, 1964. Age, 90

HERBERT HOOVER was the first President to be elected from a state west of the Mississippi; he was also the first Quaker and the first professional engineer to hold the office. Hoover was born in Iowa, the son of a village blacksmith. After the death of his parents, he was brought up by an uncle in Oregon, and it was here he developed his interest in mining engineering. He worked his way through Stanford University and soon got a chance to work in the office of a San Francisco engineer where his ability was quickly recognized, and he was entrusted with important engineering projects both in the United States and abroad.

When World War I broke out in 1914 Hoover was in London, and he immediately took up the work of helping stranded Americans. Later he became chairman of the Belgium Relief Commission, and in 1917 Wilson appointed him Federal Food Administrator. He was Secretary of Commerce under both Harding and Coolidge. In 1928 the Republicans chose him as their candidate for the Presidency when Coolidge "did not choose" to run.

Hoover entered office on the crest of prosperity, but in October, 1929, the boom burst with a stock-market crash that rocked the nation. Businesses failed, banks closed their doors, and mil-

lions were thrown out of work. The depression was world wide. Hoover organized the Reconstruction Finance Corporation to help check the decline, and proposed various other measures for relief and Federal work projects. However, Congress now turned against him and the public blamed him for the depression. In the presidential campaign of 1932 he was defeated by Franklin D. Roosevelt.

After his retirement, Hoover continued active in public service and humanitarian work. President Truman called on him to head the European Food Program in 1946, and in 1953–55 he was chairman of the committee to reorganize the U.S. Executive Departments. He died in 1964.

PUBLIC CAREER

Chairman of American Relief Committee; chairman of Commission for Relief in Belgium; U.S. Food Administrator; chairman of European Relief Council; Secretary of Commerce; President.

ADMINISTRATION EVENTS

1929 Federal Farm Board created
Stock market crash
1930 Veterans Administration created
1931 Moratorium of war debts arranged
1932 Reconstruction Finance Corporation created
1933 Twentieth Amendment ratified

BORN: March 29, 1875
BIRTHPLACE: Waterloo, Iowa
PARENTS: Charles and Florence Weed Henry
MARRIED: Herbert Hoover, 1899
CHILDREN: 2 sons
DIED: January 7, 1944. Age, 68

Lou Hoover

Maiden Name : Lou Henry

LOU HENRY and Herbert Hoover first became acquainted at Stanford University, in a geology class in which she was the only girl student. Lou Henry, like Hoover, had been born in Iowa, and she had always loved outdoor life. Her father, a banker, had brought her up almost as if she had been a boy, taking her on camping and hunting trips, and teaching her woodcraft and nature lore. The family later moved to Monterey, Cal., and she attended a normal school at San José and also classes at Stanford University, where she met Hoover. After he graduated in 1895 they became engaged, but agreed to wait until he was earning a better salary before being married. Within four years he had a good position with a London concern, and when he was offered the chance to go to China as director general of mines, he immediately cabled Lou, asking her to marry him. She agreed at once, and on Feb. 11, 1899, they were married at Monterey and sailed for China together.

The Boxer Rebellion was going on at this time, and the Hoovers were in Tientsin when the rebels attacked the city. Lou Hoover helped with the nursing and distribution of food, and showed herself cool and courageous in every emergency. In 1901 they returned to London, but later she accompanied her husband to practically every part of the world on his various business trips. Their two sons were born in London, but Lou always considered California her real home.

At the outbreak of World War I, Mrs. Hoover took her two sons to California, then rejoined her husband in London to help with relief work. After Hoover was recalled to the United States to act as Food Administrator and later as Secretary of Commerce, they made their home in Washington. During these years Mrs. Hoover was elected president of the Girl Scouts, and took an active part in raising money and building up the membership. She often took groups of girls out on hikes and camping trips.

It was just thirty years after their marriage that President and Mrs. Hoover moved into the White House. As the wife of a man who had long been a celebrity, Lou Hoover had no difficulty with her new position as First Lady. She was poised, kind, and dignified, and enjoyed meeting visitors of many different kinds.

When President Hoover was defeated for reelection in 1932, they retired to their permanent home in Palo Alto, Calif., and it was here that Mrs. Hoover died Jan. 7, 1944.

The only thing we have to fear is fear itself. . . . . In the field of world policy I would dedicate this nation to the policy of the good neighbor.

—FIRST INAUGURAL ADDRESS

Franklin Delano Roosevelt

32nd President, 1933–1945 — Party: Democratic

BORN: January 30, 1882
BIRTHPLACE: Hyde Park, New York
PARENTS: James and Sara Delano Roosevelt
EDUCATION: Harvard University
RELIGION: Episcopalian

OCCUPATION: Lawyer
MARRIED: Anna Eleanor Roosevelt, 1905
AGE AT INAUGURATION: 51
TERMS OF OFFICE: Three (12 years, 39 days)
DIED: April 12, 1945. Age, 63

FRANKLIN DELANO ROOSEVELT, our "New Deal" President, remained in office longer than any other President. He served three terms, and was elected for a fourth.

Franklin Roosevelt was related to Theodore Roosevelt, and like him, came from a wealthy New York family. He graduated from Harvard, and then studied law. He went into politics, served as a state senator, and was Assistant Secretary of Navy under President Wilson. Then in 1921, when he was 39 years old, he was stricken with infantile paralysis which left his legs crippled. With tremendous determination he set out to overcome this handicap, and in 1928 and 1930 he was elected Governor of New York.

In 1932 Roosevelt became the candidate for the Democratic party with his pledge of a "New Deal," and won the election. He immediately started on a widesweeping program to combat the depression with government works projects, relief grants, and controls over business, agriculture, and industry. The gold standard was abandoned and banks put under close Federal supervision. All of this meant a great expansion of the power of the Federal government, which was challenged as unconstitutional by many.

In 1936 Roosevelt was elected for a second term and continued his New Deal program. In 1939 World War II broke out in Europe and brought new problems. The United States proclaimed its neutrality, but national sentiment favored the Allies. In 1940 Roosevelt broke with tradition by running for a third term. On Dec. 7, 1941, the Japanese attacked Pearl Harbor and the United States officially declared war.

The President was now given almost unlimited powers. He attended many conferences abroad and helped plan for a post-war United Nations organization. In 1944 he was elected for a fourth term, but died suddenly at Warm Springs, Ga., on April 12, 1945, and was buried at Hyde Park.

PUBLIC CAREER

New York state senator; Governor of New York; Assistant Secretary of Navy; President.

ADMINISTRATION EVENTS

1933 Enactment of "New Deal" recovery measures
Twenty-first Amendment (Prohibition) repealed
1934 Philippine Independence Act passed
1935 Social Security Act passed
1937 Controversy over "packing" of Supreme Court
1939 World War II begins
1941 U. S. declares war
1942 Invasion of North Africa by Allies
1943 Invasion of Africa
1944 Invasion of France

BORN: October 11, 1884
BIRTHPLACE: New York, New York
PARENTS: Elliott and Anna Livingston Hall Roosevelt
MARRIED: Franklin Delano Roosevelt, 1905
CHILDREN: 5 sons, 1 daughter
DIED: November 7, 1962. Age, 78

Eleanor Roosevelt

Maiden Name : Anna Eleanor Roosevelt

ELEANOR ROOSEVELT was a member of the widespread Roosevelt clan which also included her future husband, Franklin Delano Roosevelt. Her father, Elliott Roosevelt, was a younger brother of Theodore Roosevelt. Her parents died when she was quite young, and Eleanor and her two brothers were brought up by their Grandmother Hall, who saw that she received a thorough education. As a girl she was awkward and shy, and social activities were an ordeal for her. But she met her distant cousin, Franklin Delano Roosevelt, when he was a senior at Harvard, and they became engaged. The marriage took place on March 17, 1905, when she was twenty years old.

During the following years while Franklin was beginning his political career, Eleanor was busy with her home and family. Six children were born to them, five boys and one girl. During the years of World War I, when Franklin was Assistant Secretary of the Navy, she devoted much of her time and energy to war work, and later, when he was Governor of New York, she became actively interested in politics. When her husband was stricken with infantile paralysis, she did much to help his recovery by keeping up his interest in public affairs. She entertained her husband's political associates, and became active in the State Democratic Committee. When he was elected Governor of New York she continued her political work, took an active part in various welfare programs, and also taught civics at the Todhunter School in New York, of which she was the vice principal.

As First Lady, after Roosevelt became President, Eleanor was even busier. Perhaps more than any other President's wife, she kept up an independent public life of her own. She traveled abroad, went on lecture tours, wrote newspaper and magazine articles, and talked over the radio. Many of her activities, of course, were for the purpose of gathering reports for her husband. Her independence of tradition and precedent caused much criticism, but her genuine sympathy and kindness were generally recognized. She was especially interested in social reforms and the problems of international peace.

After President Roosevelt's death she continued her work for these causes. To the end of her life in 1962 she was one of the foremost American women in national and international affairs.

*If we falter in our leadership
we may endanger the peace of the world,
and we shall surely endanger
the welfare of the nation.*

—MESSAGE TO CONGRESS, 1947

Harry S. Truman

33rd President, 1945-1953 — Party: Democratic

BORN: May 8, 1884
BIRTHPLACE: Lamar, Missouri
PARENTS: John Anderson and Martha Young Truman
EDUCATION: Public schools
RELIGION: Baptist

OCCUPATIONS: Businessman; lawyer
MARRIED: Elizabeth Wallace, 1919
AGE AT INAUGURATION: 60
TERMS OF OFFICE: Two (7 years, 9 months)

HARRY S. TRUMAN, who succeeded to the Presidency when Franklin Roosevelt died, hails from Missouri. His father was a farmer and livestock dealer, and Harry grew up as a farm boy. He had hoped to go to West Point, but was rejected for poor eyesight. Disappointed in this, he remained on his father's farm, but also joined a National Guard unit, and when the United States went to war with Germany in 1917 he was commissioned a lieutenant of field artillery. He served one year overseas, and returned home with the rank of major.

Truman, now married, opened a clothing store in Kansas City, but after two years it failed. Seeking a new career, he studied law and began to enter local politics. Although associated with the powerful "Boss" Prendergast at this time, Truman's own record was completely honest, and he was eventually elected to the U. S. Senate. He served in the Senate for 10 years and won recognition for his work on several important committees, particularly the Truman Committee, set up to check waste in defense expenditures. As a result, he was nominated for Vice President by the Democrats in 1944.

Less than three months after the inauguration in 1945, Truman became President. The World War II was in its final stages. In May Germany collapsed. In August, in order to hasten the end of the war, President Truman authorized the use of the atomic bomb at Hiroshima, and Japan surrendered.

Truman now was faced with many problems as the nation tried to readjust itself to peace conditions. There were serious strikes and struggles over price controls and fear of unemployment. World affairs too were in a grave condition, with the European nations exhausted. The Republicans confidently expected to win the election of 1948, but Truman put on a fighting campaign and won a surprise victory. During this term of office the Communists attacked Korea, and Truman sent forces to support the Korean Republic. Truman did not run for re-election in 1952, and retired to his home in Independence, Mo.

PUBLIC CAREER

Army officer; county judge; U. S. Senator; Vice President; President.

ADMINISTRATION EVENTS

1945 United Nations Charter signed in San Francisco
Surrender of Germany and Japan
1949 North Atlantic Treaty signed
1950 U. S. forces sent to Korea
1951 Twenty-second Amendment ratified
1952 Puerto Rico declared a Commonwealth

BORN: February 13, 1885
BIRTHPLACE: Independence, Missouri
PARENTS: David and Madge Gates Wallace
MARRIED: Harry Truman, 1919
CHILDREN: 1 daughter

Bess Truman

Maiden Name : Elizabeth Virginia Wallace

ALTHOUGH christened Elizabeth Virginia Wallace, Mrs. Truman has been called "Bess" since her childhood, and it is by this name that Americans know her best. She was born in Independence, Mo., the daughter of a banker, and came to know Harry Truman during her schooldays there. This boy-and-girl acquaintanceship ripened into an engagement in 1917, and they were married two years later, on June 28, 1919, after Truman's return from his army service in Europe.

The Trumans continued to live in Independence until 1934, when Truman was elected to the U. S. Senate. During these early years they had little money and had to live very economically while Truman was paying off the debt for his clothing store. Their one child, a daughter, was born in 1924. Bess Truman was always a devoted wife and home-maker, and when her husband became a Senator she also became his secretary, taking charge of his personal mail and going over his speeches. Then, in 1944, Truman was elected Vice President and in 1945 became President.

While ordinarily of a retiring nature, Bess Truman performed her duties as First Lady efficiently and cheerfully. All three of the Trumans love music and enjoy attending concerts whenever possible. Margaret Truman studied to become a concert singer, and made her professional debut with the Detroit Symphony Orchestra in 1947.

After the election of 1948, it was found that the White House needed very extensive repairs, and the Truman family moved to the Blair House nearby. The work of restoring and modernizing the White House took 3½ years and cost over five million dollars. There was some talk in Congress of tearing down the old building entirely, but public opinion was strongly in favor of saving as much of the historic structure as possible. The original shell was kept, but new foundations were put in, new walls raised, and all the rooms, of course, completely redecorated. Air conditioning was installed throughout the building, the kitchen was completely modernized, a broadcasting room added on the ground floor, and many other improvements made.

Bess Truman was mistress of the new White House for only a few months, since President Truman did not seek another term of office. After the inauguration ceremonies for President Eisenhower in January, 1953, Bess Truman welcomed the opportunity to return to Independence, Mo.

*The future of this republic is in
the hands of the American voter.*
—ADDRESS, 1949

Dwight David Eisenhower

34th President, 1953–1961 — Party: Republican

BORN: October 14, 1890
BIRTHPLACE: Denison, Texas
PARENTS: David J. and Ida Stoever Eisenhower
EDUCATION: West Point Military Academy
RELIGION: Presbyterian

OCCUPATION: Army officer
MARRIED: Mary Geneva Doud, 1916
AGE AT INAUGURATION: 62
TERMS OF OFFICE: Two (8 years)

DWIGHT D. EISENHOWER was the first President of our Union of 50 states. Both Hawaii and Alaska were added to the Union during his Presidency. He was also a soldier president who had had no previous political experience. Eisenhower was born in Texas but grew up in Abilene, Kans. His parents were poor but deeply religious, and brought their seven sons up strictly. He won an appointment to West Point and was graduated with high rank in 1915. He was then stationed at various army posts, at home and abroad, and from 1935 to 1939 was assistant to Gen. MacArthur in the Philippines.

After the United States entered World War II in 1941, he was assigned to the War Plans Division of the War Dept., where he worked out the plans for Allied operations in Europe. In 1942 and 1943 he directed the invasions of Africa and Italy. As Supreme Commander of the Allied forces in 1944, he directed the D-Day invasion of Normandy, and a year later received the surrender of the German army. He then returned to the United States to succeed General Marshall as U. S. Chief of Staff.

For a brief period he severed his connection with the army to become president of Columbia University, but when the North Atlantic Treaty Organization was set up in 1950 to resist Russian aggression he was recalled to act as Supreme Allied Commander. Because of his accomplishments, the Republican party drafted him to become their presidential candidate in 1952, and he won the election.

As President, Eisenhower worked constantly for peace. He brought about an armistice in the Korean War, strengthened the NATO, and took part in important international conferences. In national matters he generally followed a middle-of-the-road course. Congressional elections resulted in the Democrats controlling Congress, yet Eisenhower's personal popularity was so great that he easily won re-election in 1956. His second term of office was marked by increasing world tension, especially with Russia.

PUBLIC CAREER

Army officer; Commander in Chief, Allied Forces in Africa; Supreme Commander, Allied Expeditionary Forces; General of the Army; Chief of Staff; President.

ADMINISTRATION EVENTS

1953 Korean War ended
1955 Geneva Conference
1957 United States proposes ban on nuclear tests
First Soviet Sputnik launched
1958 First U. S. satellite launched
1959 Alaska and Hawaii admitted to Union

BORN: November 14, 1896
BIRTHPLACE: Boone, Iowa
PARENTS: John and Elivera Sheldon Doud
MARRIED: Dwight David Eisenhower, 1916
CHILDREN: 2 sons

Mamie Eisenhower

Maiden Name: Mary Geneva Doud

JUST call me Mamie," Mrs. Eisenhower said, when friends began to address her more formally after the election of her husband to the Presidency, and Mamie she has remained ever since. Her informal and democratic ways have won her a popularity almost as great as that of the President.

Mary Geneva Doud was born in 1896 in Boone, Iowa, where her father was a prosperous meat packer. When she was nine years old, however, her parents moved to Denver, where she grew up and attended school. She first met Dwight Eisenhower in 1915 at Fort Sam Houston, Tex., when he was stationed there after being graduated from West Point. The young lieutenant promptly fell in love with the pretty, light-hearted Mamie, and they were soon engaged. In 1916 they were married in Mamie's home in Denver.

They began their married life in the simple two-room officers' quarters provided at Fort Sam Houston, but as Eisenhower was constantly transferred from one post to another, Mamie had to become accustomed to making a home under all sorts of conditions and in many different parts of the world. Two sons were born to them. The first died at Fort Mead when only three years old, but the second son, John, is now grown.

When the Eisenhowers moved into the White House in 1953 they found a beautiful new building, for it had been completely remodeled and modernized during Truman's administration.

In spite of the fact that she lived abroad a great deal, Mamie Eisenhower has remained thoroughly American in her tastes. She likes American styles and American foods, and is completely natural and unaffected in her manners. With her years of experience as the wife of a high army officer, she is completely at home either at formal or informal occasions.

In 1950 the Eisenhowers bought a 189-acre farm near Gettysburg, Pa., as a home when the time came for the President to retire. The planning and furnishing of this home—the first really permanent home of their married life—has of course been of special interest to Mamie Eisenhower. During the busy years of the Presidency, it formed a quiet retreat for weekends, and it now offers a promise of future peace.

We stand today on the edge of a new frontier,
a frontier of unknown opportunities and perils,
a frontier of unfulfilled hopes and threats.
—NOMINATION ACCEPTANCE SPEECH, 1960

John Fitzgerald Kennedy

35th President, 1961-1963 — Party: Democratic

BORN: May 29, 1917
BIRTHPLACE: Brookline, Massachusetts
PARENTS: Joseph P. and Rose Fitzgerald Kennedy
EDUCATION: Harvard University
RELIGION: Catholic

OCCUPATION: Politician
MARRIED: Jacqueline Lee Bouvier, 1953
AGE AT INAUGURATION: 43
TERM OF OFFICE: 2 years, 10 months.
DIED: November 22, 1963. Age, 46

JOHN KENNEDY was the youngest man to attain the Presidency since Theodore Roosevelt, who was not quite 43 when he was sworn into office after the death of President McKinley. Kennedy was born to a family noted both for its wealth and its interest in politics. His father had made a vast fortune in various fields of business, and had also served as Ambassador to England just before World War II.

John Kennedy was the second oldest son in a family of nine children. He was educated at public schools and then went to Harvard University.

After the United States entered the war, John Kennedy joined the Navy and was in command of a torpedo patrol boat in the Pacific that was sunk by a Japanese destroyer. After the close of the war Kennedy tried newspaper work for a time, but was more attracted to politics. He was also influenced by the family feeling that he should continue the political career of his elder brother, who had been killed in the war. Although a complete amateur as a politician, he was elected to the U.S. House of Representatives in 1946 and was re-elected in 1948 and 1950, and then in 1952 he ran for Senator on the Democratic ticket against Henry Cabot Lodge. Again he was successful, and in 1958 he was re-elected.

In 1953 John Kennedy was married to Jacqueline Lee Bouvier, daughter of a wealthy New York family.

In the 1960 Democratic national convention, Kennedy won the nomination for the Presidency, in spite of objections to his youth from some of the rival candidates. His Republican opponent was Vice President Richard Nixon, and one of the novel features of the campaign was a series of television debates between the two candidates.

Soon after his inauguration he was faced with crises in Cuba, in Laos, and in Berlin. The climax came in October, 1962, when Kennedy forced Premier Khrushchev to withdraw missiles he was installing in Cuba. In domestic affairs, Kennedy pressed Congress for passage of his "New Frontier" legislative program, including tax reforms and broad civil rights bills. Neither, however, had been passed at the time of his death.

On Friday, Nov. 22, 1963, while riding through the streets of Dallas, Texas, President Kennedy was shot and killed. The assassination shocked the country, and eulogies from all quarters expressed the grief of the world over the loss of a dynamic and beloved national leader.

PUBLIC CAREER

Lieutenant, U. S. Navy; U. S. Representative; U. S. Senator; President.

BORN: July 28, 1929
BIRTHPLACE: Southampton, L. I.
PARENTS: John L. and Janet Lee Bouvier
MARRIED: John F. Kennedy, 1953
 Aristotle Onassis, 1968
CHILDREN: 1 son, 1 daughter (1 son, deceased)

Jacqueline Kennedy

Maiden Name : Jacqueline Lee Bouvier

MRS. JOHN KENNEDY, who was the youngest First Lady since Frances Folsom Cleveland, brought to the White House a tradition of gracious living. The daughter of John Bouvier III, a Wall Street broker, she was of French descent and grew up in New York and Long Island amid surroundings of wealth and social distinction. After attending private schools, she went to Vassar College for two years, and then spent a year at the Sorbonne in Paris. On her return to the United States she took her B. A. at George Washington University. Already fluent in French, Spanish, and Italian, she thought of studying for the foreign service, and she was also interested in journalism. After her graduation from George Washington she worked for a time for the Washington *Times Herald* as an "inquiring camera girl," interviewing interesting people.

In 1951, when she was 22 years old, she met John Kennedy, then a member of the House of Representatives. This was shortly before he entered the race against Henry Cabot Lodge for a seat in the Senate. Kennedy won the election in November, 1952, and on Sept. 12, 1953, he and Jacqueline Bouvier were married.

As the wife of a hard-working and hard-fighting politician, Jacqueline Kennedy had always felt that her role should be that of a homemaker, creating a restful and relaxing background for her husband. While Kennedy was in the Senate, they lived in a red brick Colonial house in Georgetown, near Washington, where she happily devoted herself to the care of her daughter, Caroline. A son was born in November, 1960.

Although Jacqueline Kennedy had never had any desire to take an active part in politics, she had frequently accompanied her husband on campaign trips and had proved to be a gracious guest at teas, luncheons, and political meetings. Her fluency in foreign languages had frequently made it possible for her to greet special groups in their own tongue. In her short occupancy in the White House, she redecorated and refurnished much of the interior.

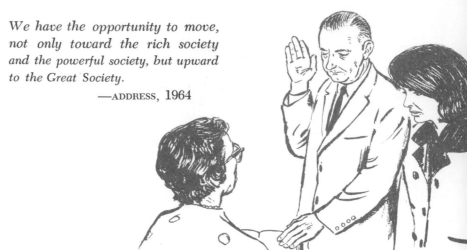

We have the opportunity to move, not only toward the rich society and the powerful society, but upward to the Great Society.

—ADDRESS, 1964

Lyndon Baines Johnson

36th President, 1963–1969 — Party: Democratic

BORN: August 27, 1908
BIRTHPLACE: Gillespie County, Texas
PARENTS: Sam Ealy and Rebekah Baines Johnson
EDUCATION: Southwest Texas State Teachers College; Georgetown University

RELIGION: Christian Church
OCCUPATION: Teacher, politician
MARRIED: Claudia Alta Taylor, 1934
AGE AT INAUGURATION: 55
TERM OF OFFICE: One (5 years, 2 months)

LYNDON BAINES JOHNSON became the eighth Vice President to succeed to the Presidency when an assassin's bullet ended the life of John F. Kennedy on November 22, 1963. He was the first President from the South in almost a century.

Johnson sprang from a long line of Texans; his father and grandfather served in the Texas House of Representatives. His mother's ancestors included Baptist ministers and educators.

Johnson worked his way through Southwest Texas State Teachers College, and then briefly taught public speaking and debating. In 1931, however, he gave up teaching to accompany Richard M. Kleberg of King Ranch fame to Congress as his secretary. This proved to be the turning point of his career. Six years later, he became a Congressman from Texas himself.

In Washington, Johnson's work habits caught the eye of President Franklin D. Roosevelt, who appointed him Texas director of the National Youth Administration in 1935. Another notable Texan, Sam Rayburn, became the constant adviser of Johnson when he was elected to the House.

In World War II Johnson was the first member of the House to go on active duty, and he returned eight months later with the rank of Lieutenant Commander in the Navy.

Johnson was first elected to the Senate in 1948. Four years later he was the Senate minority leader, and with the shift of the majority in Congress during Eisenhower's administration he became the Senate majority leader.

A seemingly tireless worker, Lyndon Johnson suffered a moderately severe heart attack in 1955. He made a remarkable comeback and went on to seek the Democratic Presidential nomination in 1960, but was defeated by John F. Kennedy. At the request of Mr. Kennedy, Johnson then accepted the nomination for the Vice Presidency.

After becoming President, Johnson continued the Kennedy policies and put through the tax reduction and civil rights measures. In 1964 he campaigned for the Presidency and won a sweeping victory over his Republican opponent, Barry Goldwater. He announced plans for government action in a "war against poverty" and for bringing about his proposed "Great Society." Foreign and domestic affairs became increasingly grave in the last years of his term, in particular the war in South Vietnam and the unrest in America's cities. In March of 1968 he announced his decision not to run for a second term.

PUBLIC CAREER

U.S. Representative; Lieutenant Commander, U.S. Navy; U.S. Senator; Vice President; President.

BORN: December 22, 1912
BIRTHPLACE: Karnack, Texas
PARENTS: Thomas and Minnie Pattillo Taylor
MARRIED: Lyndon B. Johnson, 1934
CHILDREN: Two daughters

Claudia Johnson

Maiden Name : Claudia Alta Taylor

A FAMILY servant called her Lady Bird, and ever since the name had remained. Born Claudia Alta Taylor, to a wealthy rancher and his wife, Lady Bird lost her mother at five, and grew to young womanhood among a family of men.

Shyness prevented her from calling a young man suggested by a friend to show her around the town when she visited Washington in the early summer of 1934. But fate was to have its way. Lyndon B. Johnson met Lady Bird later that summer, and on November 17 of that year they were married. Mrs. Johnson often remarked it had been her husband who helped her overcome her retiring ways. She said, "He saw more in me than I saw in myself."

Behind her early shyness lay a practical bent which led her to equip herself for several careers. To the skills of shorthand and typing she added courses in journalism and education at the University of Texas. She also qualified as a second-grade teacher.

With gentle manners and southern charm Lady Bird had been a veritable shadow of her husband since their marriage, when he was still the personal secretary of a Texas Congressman. Soon after their wedding, as her husband ran for the House and then the Senate, their pace of living quickened. For almost thirty years she had accompanied him on his campaigns and tours.

Besides being an experienced political campaigner, Lady Bird Johnson was also a clear-headed businesswoman and an executive of no mean ability. Having been left a moderate fortune by her family, she had built this into a million-dollar estate which includes a radio and TV station as well as real-estate holdings and the LBJ Ranch.

Over the years Mrs. Johnson had combined active management of these family businesses with her other duties as the mother of two lovely daughters, Lynda Bird and Lucy Baines; manager of a Washington and Texas home; and wife and hostess to a very active political figure. Probably Mrs. Johnson's greatest contribution as First Lady was her wide-ranging campaign to beautify the cities and park lands of the United States.

*America is a great nation today,
not because of what Government did for the people,
but because of what people did for themselves
over 190 years in this country.*

—NOMINATION ACCEPTANCE SPEECH, 1968

Richard Milhous Nixon

37th President, 1969-   *—Party: Republican*

BORN: January 9, 1913
BIRTHPLACE: Yorba Linda, California
PARENTS: Frank and Hannah Milhous Nixon
EDUCATION: Whittier College; Duke University

RELIGION: Quaker
OCCUPATION: Attorney
MARRIED: Patricia Ryan, 1940
AGE AT INAUGURATION: 56

RICHARD MILHOUS NIXON, after being defeated for the Presidency in 1960, made one of the most remarkable comebacks in American politics to win the Republican nomination and then the Presidential election in 1968.

Richard Nixon was the second of five sons in the family of Frank and Hannah Nixon. He was born in the village of Yorba Linda, California, but spent most of his boyhood in Whittier. The Nixons were Quakers, and Richard received a strict upbringing. After attending Whittier College, a Quaker institution, he studied law at Duke University, and returned to Whittier in 1937 to practice. There he met Patricia Ryan, a schoolteacher, and they were married in 1940. In World War II Nixon joined the Navy, and spent 15 months with the South Pacific Combat Air Transport Command. After his discharge in 1946 he entered politics, and was elected to the U.S. House of Representatives. In 1950 he ran for the Senate and won a seat there.

During his years in the House, Nixon won national recognition for his role on the House Un-American Activities Committee. By 1952 many of the party leaders felt that he would make an ideal Vice-Presidential candidate to run with General Dwight D. Eisenhower.

As Vice-President, Nixon took a more active part in the government than any other Vice-President for generations. He presided at meetings of the Cabinet and the National Security Council when President Eisenhower was ill, and he made goodwill trips as President Eisenhower's personal representative to the Far East, to South America, and to various European countries, including the Soviet Union. President Eisenhower said of him: "No man in history was ever better trained for the Presidency."

In 1960, Vice-President Nixon was nominated as the Republican candidate for the Presidency, opposing Democratic Senator John Kennedy of Massachusetts. Nixon was defeated in the closest national election since 1880.

Nixon then returned to California and in 1962 ran for governor, but was again defeated. Out of politics, he went back to the practice of law, but continued to support Republican candidates. In 1968 he was once again the nominee for President. In an extremely close and exciting election he defeated his Democratic opponent, Vice-President Hubert H. Humphrey, and George Wallace, the American Independent Party nominee, to become the 37th President.

PUBLIC CAREER

Lt. Commander, U.S. Navy; U.S. Representative;
U.S. Senator; Vice-President; President.

BORN: March 16, 1912
BIRTHPLACE: Ely, Nevada
PARENTS: William and Kate Ryan
MARRIED: Richard Nixon, June 21, 1940
CHILDREN: Two daughters

Patricia Nixon

Maiden Name : Thelma Catherine Patricia Ryan

PATRICIA NIXON has had a long, thorough preparation for her new role as First Lady of the White House. She has shared her husband's political career from the beginning, and has been a devoted and tireless partner in all his activities.

Mrs. Nixon was born in the town of Ely, Nev., and was named Thelma Catherine Patricia Ryan. Her birthdate was March 16, but her father, a loyal Irishman, took to calling her Pat and celebrating her birthday on St. Patrick's Day, and this has become a family custom. When she was a year old her parents moved to a farm near Artesia, Calif., where she grew up. Her mother died when she was 13 years old and her father when she was 17, and from then on she was self-supporting. Ambitious for a college education, she worked her way through the University of Southern California and graduated with a *cum laude* degree in 1937.

She then took a teaching position in Whittier, Calif., where Richard Nixon had just begun his career as an attorney. Nixon heard of the attractive young teacher and joined the local little theater group in order to meet her. He impulsively proposed to her the first night they met, but it took two years of persistent courtship before she finally accepted him. They were married on June 21, 1940, and their first home was an apartment over a garage. Patricia kept on with her teaching, but when Nixon went to Washington at the beginning of the war, she went with him, and later, while he was overseas, she worked in a government office in San Francisco.

From the beginning of Nixon's political career, Patricia worked shoulder to shoulder with him. In all his campaigns she accompanied her husband and took an active part in political affairs. As wife of the Vice-President, she accompanied him on his world travels. Her tactfulness and charm of manner as well as her unfailing social poise and her remarkable physical stamina are a constant marvel to her associates. During the Washington years, she won acclaim as one of the most capable and popular hostesses in capital history.

The Nixons have two daughters, Patricia and Julie, and in spite of her many public and social activities, Mrs. Nixon has been a devoted mother.

Index

PRINTED IN U.S.A.